THE

O

FACTOR

IDENTIFYING AND DEVELOPING
5- TO 25-YEAR-OLDS WHO ARE GIFTED IN
ORGANIZATIONAL LEADERSHIP

ALAN E. NELSON, ED.D.

Let's develop leaders in Coolio Valley!

Summit Crest Publishing
Fort Collins, CO

Copyright © 2016 Alan E. Nelson

ISBN-13: 978-1523483846
ISBN-10: 1523483849

What experts are saying...

Parents and teachers often ask me for advice about developing leadership in children and youth. From here on out, I will refer them to this tremendously helpful book, filled with clear insight about leadership as an "O factor" and how to nurture and develop leadership. This is a most important book; any parent or teacher who cares about raising or developing morally responsible leaders must read it. A truly inspiring book.

-Dr. Dorothy Sisk, Conn Chair in Gifted Education, Lamar University, Beaumont, Texas; Former Director of the Office of Gifted & Talented in Washington DC and author of Making Great Kids Greater

If you care about cultivating leadership qualities in kids, you can't afford to miss this remarkable book by Dr. Alan E. Nelson. Filled with an abundance of practical ideas, this book explains new and creative ways of building competence and character in the next generation.

– Les Parrott, Ph.D., Founder of RealRelationships.com, author of 3 Seconds

As a young girl, I was frequently told, "You're too bossy!" The characteristic has served me well in many respects, but could have transformed into what it really meant: a valuable leadership skill. With a program like KidLead, vice years of muddling through it on my own, this trait could have been well-honed much earlier, without negative connotation or the second guessing I put myself through. Let young women be known for what they are, not bossy, but assertive leaders.
-Krysten J. Ellis, Lt. Commander, SC, USN (1st US Naval Female Submariner)

As leadership is included in many state definitions of giftedness and talent, The O Factor provides focus for the conversation regarding leadership development. This book can aid educators and other stakeholders interested in supporting young people, who evidence advanced leadership abilities, cultivate this potential.

-Jennifer L Jolly, PhD, Senior Lecturer, Gifted Education; GERRIC Senior Research Fellow; MTeach Program Director

Practical. Relevant. Authentic. These words describe the book you have in your hand. The O Factor is a tool you can use and a reference guide you can refer to over and over again as you equip your children to be leaders. If you think your student might be a leader, this is your handbook to coach them on their journey.
-Dr. Tim Elmore, President of Growing Leaders.com, author of Habitudes

The KidLead (O Factor) training program has been a great addition to our after school programs and has enhanced our students' leadership capacity and ability to work together as a team. We are proud to be able to offer such an effective and meaningful program for our children and families.
-Dr. Laurie Corso, Principal in the Poudre School District, Colorado

Developing leadership skills and ethical behaviors are tasks that many adults struggle with. The O Factor presents a straight forward, practical guide to fostering gifted youth, who show the potential for being great leaders. This is a much needed resource for educators, parents, and community members, as we embark on finding the next generation of leaders, who can positively change our world.

Katie D. Lewis, Ed.D, Assistant Professor of Education, Texas A&M International University

Of all the domains of human ability that are discussed in the field of gifted education, none has more promise to affect greater change in the world than that of leadership. Although acknowledged as an area of talent since the 1970s, leadership talent is too often left to wither on the vine. What Dr. Alan Nelson has done is offer a model of leadership development that is based on the existing knowledge base of organizational leadership, but targeted at youth. His model, his assessments, and his personal passion for the topic make a compelling case for how and why leadership potential should be developed in K-12 youth.

-Scott J. Peters, Ph.D., Associate Professor of Educational Foundations, University of Wisconsin - Whitewater

The O Factor provides a perspective that will encourage parents and educators to take a fresh view at leadership and opportunities to develop leadership potential.

-Julia Link Roberts, Mahurin Professor of Gifted Studies; Executive Director, The Center for Gifted Studies and The Carol Martin Gatton Academy of Mathematics and Science, Western Kentucky University

The O Factor provides an effective framework and paradigm for both parents and educators in identifying and understanding extraordinary and innate leadership abilities exhibited by certain youth. More importantly, the book outlines practical strategies that can be used to develop natural leadership gifts and talents in children and young people. There are many meaningful applications and implications for families, educators, school environments, student leadership programs, and most of all those being nurtured, developed and served in these systems.

-JJ Colburn, CAE Executive Director
Texas Association for the Gifted & Talented

As a teacher and parent of gifted students with leadership ability, I found "The O Factor: Identifying and Developing Students Gifted in Leadership Ability" to be insightful and engaging. Dr. Nelson's use of authentic examples drew me in as a reader and encouraged me to reflect on the gifted leaders I teach and parent. With a great balance of theory and practical strategies for identifying and supporting students with the "O Factor," this book is definitely a must-read for all teachers and parents!

Katherine B. Brown, Ph.D., Enrichment Specialist, Judia Jackson Harris Elementary School and Adjunct Assistant Professor, University of Georgia, Athens, GA

The O Factor tells us why and how to recognize and mentor leadership talent in ages 10-13. It is a great guide to parents and adults to work with youth.

- Lois F. Roets Ed.D., Author: *Leadership: Skills Training Programs for Ages 8-18.* www.RoetsNotes.com

A progressive society is one that is keenly interested in the state of its future generations. The O Factor is a must-read for anyone who desires to cultivate the next generation of leaders for a more just, peaceful, and sustainable world. Dr. Nelson's pioneering work instills vision, hope, and practical steps for developing effective and ethical young leaders. With a sense of urgency, I wholeheartedly recommend this book to anyone who is serious about leadership development.

-Shuang Frances Wu, Ph.D., Assistant Professor of Leadership, Azusa Pacific University, Azusa, CA

I think it is invaluable to begin teaching leadership to kids. That's when we're going to influence them for a lifetime of leading. I've been working with national leaders for years, and I believe that the best time to begin training them is when they are young.

– John Kotter, DBA, Harvard professor emeritus and bestselling author of "Leading Change" and "A Sense of Urgency"

Dedication

This book is dedicated to my wife, one of the finest leaders I've ever met and who at a very young age was identified as an O Factor. She led in high school, college and at 25, leadership guru John Maxwell hired her to be on his leadership team. She's still leading in her industry today. It's also dedicated to Juniper Nelson, the most darling granddaughter a family could desire.

I also want to thank our growing network of global friends, dedicated to identifying and developing students possessing The O Factor. I am honored to work with people such as Arinya Talerngsri (Thailand), Dr. Lagan Gill (India), Ileana Gonzales (Peru), Paul Zyntek (Australia), Justine Cambell (Hong Kong), Nicki Straza (Canada), Dr. Kong (Korea), Hafsa Abbasy and Rahila Narejo (Pakistan), Aline Mancini (Brazil), Aman Merchant (UAE), and Dr. Frances Wu and Xueyan Gao (China) who represent the high caliber of professionals being drawn to the concept of a young leader revolution.

Author's Note:

This book is a significant update of "How to Bring Out the Leader in Your Child," offering insights from the fields of gifted and talents as well as school climate and positive behavior.

The O Factor

Table of Contents

Preface

From the Author's Heart:

For some of you, this may be the most important book you read in terms of life impact. Whether you're a parent or a professional who works with 2- to 22-year olds potentially gifted in leadership, the ability to understand the O Factor is very significant. I call it "life math." When you're a good person and/or develop talented people, you add to life. When you're a leader, you multiply. But when you're someone who develops young leaders, you possess exponential influence with what you do. In other words, you multiply the multipliers.

As a person who has studied leadership most of my life, collecting over 800 books on the subject, a doctorate and publishing a dozen books and over 100 articles on the topic, I'm convinced that the way we've gone about developing those who lead the organizations, governments and societies in the world is significantly flawed. We allow individuals with organizational ability to rise through the ranks, often regardless of their ethics or efficacy. The results include bankrupt corporations, countries that reduce the dignity of humanity, and disappointed masses who languish for more proficient leaders.

For the life of me, I don't know why we wait so long to identify those who possess an abundant ability to organize us, and offer unique training opportunities to develop them while they're moldable. While we've learned a lot about students gifted and talented in academics, athletics, and the arts, we're far behind in our acumen to identify and develop those who help the rest of us work together to accomplish much.

This book is written for parents, educators, and social innovators, who want to build a better world.

The two most important days of your life are the day you are born and the day you find out why.

-Mark Twain

For many, this book is about that second day, when you help our children and youth discover that their primary purpose in life is to organize the rest of us to accomplish together, what we would not or could not as individuals; who bring out the best in all of us.

If you want to improve the world, focus on leaders.

If you want to improve leaders, focus on them when they're young.

-Alan E. Nelson

Los Angeles, California

Chapter 1
What is the O Factor?

It's All Around Us

    I grew up on a farm. Every year, I'd look up in the sky and see flocks of geese heading south for the winter. They flew in a V-formation, honking sporadically, flapping their wings in unison.

As I looked across the fields, I watched herds of cattle and hogs and flocks of sheep.

 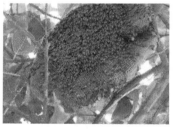

I also noticed colonies of ants and beehives.

During the spring, I noticed schools of fish and tadpoles swimming in the pond and nearby lake.

At school we watched National Geographic films showing how animals group together, whether they be herds of elephants, prides of lions, or packs of hyenas.

I also read how the Native Americans used to hunt bison. They'd go after the lead animal because once they killed it, the others stopped running, making them easy prey.

As I grew up, I studied how humans organize themselves. At times they do it for fun and entertainment.

My experience teaching at the Naval Postgraduate School taught me some of the intricacies of how we organize to protect ourselves and kill our enemies.

Animals, insects, and humans organize themselves, assigning roles to individuals for a cumulative result of synergy, whereby total output exceeds the sum of individual inputs. One of these specific roles is that of the organizer. The organizing members help the others work as a unit to achieve together what they would not or could not as individuals. This is what we refer to as the "O Factor." What is instinctual among most species is that the majority of each seek the minority of these organizers who appear to possess the O Factor naturally. At other times, those with the O Factor assert themselves and the others decide whether or not to acknowledge them. The community recognizes the importance of these specialists for greater accomplishment, whether for commerce, security, entertainment, or any number of other desirable effects.

The O Factor in Humanity

As you look at the history of humanity, the single most defining factor is the quality and character of those possessing the O Factor. The masses do not make history as much as those who organize them. Often this has been for the good!

But unfortunately, far too many of this type of people have hurt society.

One way to better understand the impact of these organizers is to analyze them in terms of how effective and ethical they are (see Graph 1.0). When those who are effective and unethical prevail, society suffers. Wars, atrocities, and abuse litter the landscape when these individuals organize us. When organizers are ethical but ineffective, the potential for good is wasted. So in this simple but practical analysis, we'd all agree that what our corporations, non-profits, schools, governments, and communities need are organizers who are both effective and ethical. How can we accomplish this?

That is the heart of this book.

High	**Ethical But Ineffective** Evil dominates if stronger	**Ethical And Effective** Good prevails
Ethics	**Unethical And Ineffective** Good dominates if stronger	**Unethical And Effective** Evil prevails
Low		

Low	**Competency**	High

Graph 1.0 Ethical versus Effective Organizers

I am not an educational, children's, or youth expert. My specialty is leadership studies. I'm interested in what it is that causes certain people to be so effective at getting others to follow them and work together to accomplish great things. Most who study what I do work with adults. But at midlife— after completing a doctorate in leadership, investing a decade in writing articles and books, and speaking at conferences and universities—I came to the conclusion that our best efforts at improving the efficacy of organizers is wasted on them after their most pliable age, both cognitively and in character. That began a significant pivot in my life to study influencers before they move into roles of significance.

Benefits of Starting Early

Imagine what it would be like if we had the ability to identify those with the O Factor at a very young age. Who would benefit from an audacious idea of developing these organizers so early?

An obvious beneficiary is the parents of O Factor students. No one is more motivated to help children than their parents, but often, parents of those with exceptional organizational skills don't know how to raise them because they are different from most. Many a well-meaning parent tries to subdue and discipline an O Factor child for being who they are: non-compliant. By better understanding these children, parents would not only raise more confident kids, but also save themselves from a lot of headaches and frustrations.

Another beneficiary of identifying and developing young people possessing the O Factor are the organizations these students occupy. A big one is schools. Classrooms, school halls, and playgrounds are already influenced by unrecognized and undeveloped O Factor students, but imagine what it would be like if we intentionally developed them to lead their peers in positive behaviors. Although educators desire the latter, they significantly underestimate the former. Research demonstrates the connection between school climate and academic achievement. Just as thermometers tell the temperature but thermostats set it, we refer to these O Factor students as *Thermostats* because they possess the ability to raise or lower the relational temperature of an organization. Unfortunately, most schools are O Factor averse, leading to frustrated students and educators.

Obviously, the benefit to the O Factor children and youth themselves is being affirmed for what they are good at and being given such a large head start in life. Malcolm Gladwell's focus on outliers—those who are exceptionally successful in their field—notes the value in experience. Doing a task 10,000 times will significantly increase a person's skill. Imagine how effective our 5-, 10-, and 15-year-olds would be after 5, 10, and 15 years of organizational leading.

But the greatest beneficiary is not the parent, the school, or even the O Factor individuals themselves, but rather society at large. By identifying and developing children and youth possessing the O Factor, we circumvent a lot of the lamentations we've experienced both historically and currently. This is in addition to the sheer numbers of organizational leaders needed globally in the coming decades. A Deloitte study report on the business sector alone noted that an inadequate leader pipeline is one of three things that keep executives awake at night. "Leadership remains the top talent issues among businesses around the world, with only 14% of companies stating they feel their leadership pipeline is 'ready.'"[1]

Successions plans are huge concerns in corporations today. Researchers Avolio and Vogelgesang note, "With a looming leadership shortage and global war for leadership talent, we cannot rely solely on organizations to train their leaders; we must begin leader development at an earlier age, developing leaders long before they even join those organizations to pursue their careers."[2] "There is an enormous individual and social cost when talent among the Nation's children and youth goes undiscovered and undeveloped. These students cannot ordinarily excel without assistance" (Marland Report, 10).[3]

What would it be like if we could identify individuals with the O Factor at a very young age? Every good and evil leader was at one time a 10-year-old. What if we could get to them early in order to shape their values, character, and invest in their skills? Unfortunately, the way we identify and develop leaders has changed little throughout history. But we now have the social technology to re-engineer society as we know it.

By recognizing the early indicators during childhood and adolescence, we can offer specific and concentrated training, giving these young organizers a significant head start. Just as countries prospect future Olympic athletes or academic prodigies, we could select those possessing an inordinate ability to help the rest of us accomplish great things together, instead of waiting for these potential leaders long past the time of pliability and moral development. Entire nations could revamp the process by which they fill the leadership pipelines within their cultures.

My work the last decade, in observing and interacting with 1000s of children and teens around the world possessing the O Factor, convinces me that we have the potential to significantly benefit society by changing the way we develop those who organize us. That's what this book is about: the identification and development of those with the O Factor, getting to them while they're moldable, not moldy.

Clarifying the Concept

Now that we've introduced the O Factor, let's take a moment to explain the concept further. Some may be suspicious of our impetus on organizing ability. Doesn't this sound a lot like leadership? What's the difference? That's a legitimate question. The primary reason that we refer to this social behavior as the O Factor, the ability to organize others, is because the term *leadership* lacks sufficient clarity within society to define what it is that distinguishes those who truly lead. Over the years, I've owned over 800 books on leadership and have reviewed even more. Less than 5% of them defined the term they used constantly.

The word "leadership" only dates back to the early 1800s. Official study of the social process we call leadership began in the 1940s. My doctorate is from the University of San Diego, the first higher education institution to offer a doctorate in the field. Now, 100s of universities offer terminal degrees on the topic. Leadership has become a hot commodity in terms of books, seminars, degrees, articles, and social discussions. The problem is a lack of clarity of what people mean when they talk about it.

This is exceptionally challenging when you analyze leadership resources for those who focus on young people, under the age of 20. Most of the time, *leadership* refers to any number of concepts, typically referring to self-confidence, self-actualization, citizenship, self-esteem, and teamwork. Unfortunately, this is a significant difference from those who work with executives who actually lead organizations. Most who develop leadership programs for children and youth have little to no training in the field of leadership development, and have not led organizations themselves or experienced executive training. As a result, most of the content related to young leadership development is not about what leaders actually *do*.

Therefore, the O Factor refers to the unique ability possessed by a small minority to instinctually accomplish things by organizing others to work together for a common goal. By creating a term that focuses on the primary function of these people, we cut through the messiness and baggage that terms like "leadership" involve. By identifying people possessing the O Factor very young (between 5 and 18 years of age), we can intentionally develop them into superior social influencers who are both effective and ethical. The result is to improve the many organizations that make up societies around the world.

Defining Leadership

Although we'll primarily be using the term O Factor to refer to students with exceptional talents in organizing others, I want to drive our stake in the ground in terms of defining organizational leadership for the context of this book. Whenever you want to have a quality conversation with someone on leadership, make sure you define the term, since people are all over the place in what they think it is. My focus is not so much on the concept, but rather what those who lead do that makes them effective, thus my impetus on the verb.

Leading is influencing people to willfully attempt together, what they would not or could not as individuals.

* *Leadership* is the overall term for this social process.

* *Leaders* are those who lead, not just occupy a position or claim a title.

Let's break it down:

Influencing: Leading is a type of influence, activated power, although not all influence is leadership.

People: Leadership is a social process, evolving from the need to organize talents, resources, opinions, ideas, and other skills within a community. You don't lead alone. "Leading yourself" is a popular and confusing reference to other desirable qualities such as self-discipline, self-efficacy, and emotional intelligence.

13

* *Willfully*: An important qualification of leading is volition, free will. This distinguishes how leaders organize others as opposed to bullies who primarily employ coercion, a significantly different social process.

* *Attempt*: This infers that the process of leading can succeed, even if the intended objective is not obtained. History is replete with examples of great leading that failed to reach the goal and horrible leading that succeeded. While most believe that effective leadership results in far greater results than ineffective, we should distinguish producing the process from achieving its objective.

* *Would* not: This denotes social potency, the ability to persuade people to change their mind and behavior. Sometimes, individuals can achieve the same things alone, but do not. For example, a student could go to the mall after school but may not, so when a leader persuades friends to meet at the mall to hang out, that's leading.

* *Could* not: This pinpoints the power of the leadership process, in that the group experiences synergy, whereby the end result is greater than the sum total of the individual parts. There are many things in life that we cannot obtain without organizing people to synchronize their resources. Thus, we all benefit individually from the productivity of people using their unique strengths and skills. Plus, the sense of gratification and belonging that come from achieving things together offer a vital part of what makes us human.

A definition like this and list of characteristics emphasize what makes leading unique to other social behaviors often confused with leadership.

NOTE: From this point forward, we'll commonly refer to children and youth possessing the O Factor as O Factors, in order to simplify the writing and avoid wordiness of saying "a child with the O Factor." Also, we'll typically refer to children and youth as "students," since this is a simple way to span the age range of 5-18, as opposed to referring to them as children, preteens, adolescents, youth, and even young adults. We don't mean to imply a school or educational setting, but rather a common social role and title of this demographic.

Endnotes:

1. Deloitte Consulting LLP. (2014). *The Deloitte business confidence.*

2. Avolio, B. J. and Vogelgesang, G. R. "Beginnings matter in genuine leadership development" in Early Development and Leadership eds Murphy, S. E. & Reichard, R. J. (ch. 9; p 181)

3. Marland, S. P., Jr. (1972). Education of the gifted and talented: Report to the Congress of the United States by the U.S. Commissioner of Education and background papers submitted to the U.S. Office of Education, 2 vols. Washington, DC: U.S. Government Printing Office. (Government Documents Y4.L 11/2: G36)

Reference Note: Because I will be referring to the Marland Report throughout this book, a landmark study (1972) published by the US Department of Education on gifted and talented students, I will periodically cite this in the text instead of the endnotes.

Chapter 2

What if my child isn't an

O Factor?

Gifted and Talented

Many have studied what it is that makes some people so much smarter and more talented than others. In the early 1900s, Alfred Binet, a French psychologist, developed the first intelligence test in order to identify students who might need extra help in school. The Binet-Simon IQ test came to the United States and was modified by Lewis Terman, a professor at Stanford University. Variations of these assessments are still used today. In the 1940s through 1970s, psychologist J. P. Guilford did research with the US Army and at the University of Southern California. He rejected the notion of summarizing IQ with a single number, preferring to look at a variety of angles. The question changed from "How smart are you?" to "How are you smart?" This expanded notion continued with Howard Gardner's work at Harvard with multiple intelligences, published in 1983, that identified eight areas, expanding beyond the intellectual to include kinesthetic (athletic), artistic, and social. The latter, called interpersonal intelligence, included a domain he recognized as leadership. Daniel Goleman's work in the area of social intelligence (1990s) represents a related expansion.

After the 1957 launch of Russia's Sputnik rocket and satellite, the United States became anxious about identifying talent to keep pace with other countries. Subsequent emphasis on staying competitive globally with the best and brightest created interest in how to identify special gifts and talents. In 1970, a Congressional mandate resulted in a study by the US Department of Education to update the government on what was being done to identify and develop students who demonstrate exceptional abilities. In 1972 the Marland Report was published, named after the US Commissioner of Education, S. P. Marland, Jr. It listed six domains, including leadership ability.

This report is a primary document in the gifted and talented movement, as it explained types of gifts and talents, the importance of unique programs to develop these students, the state of schools regarding gifted education programs, and the potential harm and danger of not recognizing their distinctions. Many state Departments of Education in the US recognize leadership ability in their definitions of giftedness, as do numerous districts such as Los Angeles Unified School District, the nation's second largest. (Note: California tends to use the term GATE for gifted and talented education. Generally "gifted and talented" and "gifted education" are used more broadly to refer to this focus on exceptionally talented students. We'll refer to gifted and talented as GT.)

"Gifted and talented children are those identified by professionally qualified persons who by virtue of outstanding abilities, are capable of high performance. These are children who require differentiated educational programs, and/or services beyond those normally provided by the regular school program in order to realize their contribution to self and society" (Marland

Report, 20). In 1988 the federal Javits Gifted and Talented Education Act, funding gifted education research, echoed the importance of recognizing leadership ability. "These children and youth exhibit high performance capability in intellectual, creative and/or artistic areas, <u>possess an unusual leadership capacity</u>, or excel in specific academic fields. They require services and activities not ordinarily provided by schools."

So what does it mean when people talk about gifted and talented (GT)? In the past, it referred to "the really smart kids" in school, based on a single test that resulted in an intelligence quotient (IQ). Average IQ is around 100, so a child with 130 was considered moderately gifted and 160, highly gifted. This identification process changed, the more experts studied GT. Now it's based on various things, including assessments, inventories, observations, and even motivation. GT programs vary among institutions. Some consider the top 3-5% as gifted, whereas others focus on the highest 10%. Within the GT community, a variety of views exists. Some don't like the word gifted because it can infer elitism. Others prefer talent. The former implies heightened potential and the latter demonstrated development.

Most agree that GT is domain specific, meaning it's more than IQ. For example, a student who is really good at math won't automatically be good in language. In fact, exceptional students in specific areas are often quite average in other areas. One reason this is helpful when studying the O Factor is that it's easy to overlook a student who might be only average or above average academically, but have extraordinary aptitude for organizing others. We already know this is true in the area of athletics (kinesthetic intelligence), art, and other domains, so we should not confuse types of talent. An old business professor joke in higher education is to be nice to your "A" students, because they'll come back as faculty, but be very nice to your "C" students, because they'll come back to donate millions of dollars in endowments.

19

The reason it's important for educational systems to identify students with exceptional ability is that if they are not provided specialized learning opportunities, their potential will be wasted. It's the same reason we shouldn't leave behind students lacking intellectual capacity. One size doesn't fit all in life, whether it be clothes or education. But while schools emphasize the academic features of gifted and talented, who is developing the other domains? The Marland Report notes these concerns.

Gifted and talented youth are a unique population, differing markedly from their age peers in abilities, talents, interests, and psychological maturity. They are the most versatile and complex of all human groups, possibly the most neglected of all groups with special educational needs. Their sensitivity to others and insight into existing school conditions make them especially vulnerable, because of their ability to conceal their giftedness in standardized surroundings and to seek alternative outlets. The resultant waste is tragic. Research studies on special needs of the gifted and talented demonstrate the need for special programs. Contrary to widespread belief, these students cannot ordinarily excel without assistance. Developmental programs have not produced arrogant, selfish snobs; special programs have extended a sense of reality, wholesome humility, self-respect, and respect for others. A good program for the gifted increases their involvement and interest in learning through the reduction of the irrelevant and redundant (p. 42).

The fact that little has been done within schools or even the field of gifted and talented regarding leadership ability should not surprise us, because for the most part, educational systems concentrate on intellectual development. A few dabble in athleticism and the arts, but for the most part, serious leadership research and emphasis has been relegated to the world of adults, not children and youth. After all, that is where the felt need for organizational leadership is and thus where the money flows. Annually, it is estimated that billions of dollars in the US are spent on leadership development, and certainly more globally. Scores of books, courses, articles, and seminars are available on the subject.

The bottom line is that you don't need to believe the US Department of Education's definition of giftedness, or any number of lab coat-wearing, clipboard-toting scientists. Just take a few minutes peering through the fence at the nearest elementary school. See how kids organize themselves during recess. Every teacher knows that certain students possess an inordinate amount of the social influence. They're the ones who pick the teams, decide what everyone plays, and set up the games. You can see these behaviors as young as preschool and wherever children socialize. Certain kids just have the "it" factor when it comes to organizing the others to do things they normally would not or could not alone. This is what we call the O Factor.

A Weakness of Egalitarianism

By now you may be thinking, since the title of this chapter is "What if my child doesn't possess the O Factor?", why are you spending so much time talking about gifted and talented? The reason is that I want to emphasize the uniqueness of each student. Every child does not need to possess significant skills in organizing others to be successful. Rather, success is directly related to each person maximizing their potential by developing their strengths. Far too many parents want their children to follow in their footsteps. That is unfortunate. Someone said, "A child is not a book to be written, but a book to be read." Society needs the talents and constructive abilities of your child. If his or her strength is not leading others organizationally, that's okay.

The myth that everyone can lead and everyone should be taught to be a leader is just that, a myth. The social pressure to be perceived as a leader has become so strong that we can't imagine thinking of our child as not a leader. That would be a failure. Thus, we dilute the meaning of leading and leadership to the point that it fits everyone. We say it's about being a good person, or having character, or doing your best. We lower the bar so low that everyone reaches it, but then we fail to identify those with exceptional abilities to organize others to achieve things together and as a result, neglect to offer them opportunities to develop their potential.

The Marland Report points out the challenge of developing gifted and talented students in the US culture. "Educators, legislators, and parents have long puzzled over the problem of educating gifted students in a public educational program geared primarily to a philosophy of egalitarianism" (p. 6). Awhile ago, I was talking to Dr. Bill Damon in his office at Stanford University. Bill is the Director of the Stanford Center on Adolescence and teaches in the school of education. He said, "We believe in equality, more than any country in the world. But when a value goes too far, it becomes non-productive. The typical school overlooks students who are the most creative and who have the most energy to get things done." In other words, by treating everyone the same, we create vanilla people instead of bringing out their distinct flavors. One educational expert noted, "Conformity is precisely the cross upon which special education for the gifted hangs supine" (Marland Report, 69).

It's Their Success, Not Yours

So regardless of your child's abilities, s/he has the potential for success, defined by her/his aptitudes, passions, and opportunities. Whether your child is an über organizer or becomes a CEO is immaterial. We must not value our kids based on whether or not they possess the O Factor. That's an odd thing to say in a book on this topic, but when authors and leadership gurus promote ideas that are not evidenced in real life, they set us all up to fail.

Raising three sons, we spent a lot of time on ballfields and courts. We invested a lot of time and energy in sports. One year, our middle son was in Tee Ball, so I and another father volunteered to manage a team. Both of us were new at coaching, but who could mess up Tee Ball? After about three practices, one of the fathers walked over to me and asked, "Do you know who those two guys are, sitting in the grass?"

He pointed to a couple of the dads who'd been at the practices and had three kids on the team between them.

I shrugged my shoulders. "I don't know."

"That's Matt Williams and Kirt Manwaring. They're starters for the San Francisco Giants."

I had to admit that was a little intimidating. The great thing about those two pro baseball players is that they didn't put any pressure on us or their kids, unlike many other parents through the years. They knew this was just Tee Ball. They weren't trying to get their kids to follow in their footsteps. Sometimes we confuse good parenting with trying to get our kids to be like us or attempting to live out our dreams through them. A good parent probes for the potential in his or her child and then nurtures visible potential as far as possible, without performance pressure or the roar of a "Tiger Mom." Many organizational leaders want their children to be like them, because they understand the perks and benefits of these roles. Others want their kids to be the boss because they never got to be and resented it. These are understandable if not misaligned intentions for our kids.

Your child may grow up to be a brilliant scientist, an artist, engineer, or performer. He or she may be a full-time parent or chef or assist others in helping them maximize their gifts and talents. But at the end of the day and life, success is a matter of fulfilling our specific call based on how we're wired and how we discern our purpose. So this chapter is designed to let down gently those parents and educators who discover in the following chapters that their student(s) don't appear to possess the O Factor. The O Factor isn't the cure for unhappiness and will not magically make your child better than others, only different.

The cultural expression "you can be whatever you want to be," while inspiring, can also be debilitating. Everyone has both strengths and limitations. Research in positive psychology shows us that we're most apt to be successful in the areas of our strengths. Therefore, where do our gifts and talents lie and how can we develop these more effectively? Instead of dabbling in everything, what can we do to help young people discover their aptitudes early? Some dabbling may be required to find individual abilities, but for the most part, we should help our children and youth maximize their strengths sooner than later. As a 6-foot-1, slightly overweight, middle-aged male, could I play in the NBA if I wanted? Of course not. I also couldn't as a fit 20-year-old, no matter how many posters of Michael Jordan or LeBron James I glued to my refrigerator door. It's not going to happen. It's not in my genes.

People say: "But don't take our dreams away." "Don't tell people what they can't do." "When I was a child, no one would ever think I could lead anything, but now I am. What about all the kids like me you'd overlook?" These are some of the arguments I hear from adults when we introduce the idea of identifying gifted and talented leaders. Certainly, some of them warrant respect. Exceptions will always exist; we're not diminishing them. You'll always be able to find late bloomers who discover a hidden talent as an adult or who never had an opportunity to shine until later in life. The problem is that by not identifying those with observable aptitudes and strengths, we do them a larger disservice. We steal limited time and resources from developing those with measurable aptitudes, in order to help find those who may be overlooked because "you never know." It's like moving a mountain of dirt to find a few nuggets of gold here and there. We'd be better off using the skills of a geology expert to show us where to dig.

A far more effective alternative to letting everyone do what they want is to provide instruments and processes to detect early talent and then offer accelerated programs to develop it. In real life, we understand that everyone is different. Some people are great with numbers, others with art, some with people, and others athletics. Everyone who has ever worked in organizational life understands that certain people should not be put in charge of projects or people, because then everyone suffers. So why do we not think this true for children?

There's a big difference between helping students discover what they're most apt to be successful at and telling them what they won't become. This book is advocating the former, not the latter. By identifying students displaying O Factor qualities and then providing developmental opportunities specific to their potential, we offer them a huge head start. While many may grow various levels of organizational skill as they mature social-emotionally and gain experience, we should not overlook the windows of early opportunity to find those most apt to become leaders and make sure they're positioned to be effective and ethical. The goal for every child is to find their unique gifts, abilities, and interests and help them leverage these. But those possessing a special talent to organize others to achieve things should be identified and offered specialized training to catapult them forward, for their sake and that of society at large.

As we move forward, I encourage educators and those who work with children and youth to think about identifying students who may be gifted in organizational leadership. If you're a parent and you have a child under 10, you'll want to read with the intent of understanding what to look for, especially in social behaviors. Until the age of 10, when there is a significant boost in cognitive development and socio-emotional maturity, offering experiences is the best way to determine whether or not there's a talent for organizational leading. If your child is 10 or older, you should be able to tell whether or not s/he has an aptitude for organizational leadership. If so, you'll want to pursue the types of training described in this book. If after reading this book you determine that your student does not appear to have an aptitude for organizational leadership, s/he can pursue these skills later in life as others do, but be encouraged to help them discover what they are good at so they can develop these talents early.

In the next chapter, we'll look at how you can identify the organizational leadership ability and address the age-old questions, are leaders born or made?

Chapter 3

Are O Factors born or made?

The simple answer to this chapter title is, "yes."

Nature and Nurture

Recently I Googled, "Are leaders born or made?" In less than a second, the search showed over 47,000,000 results. Nature describes *what is*, and nurture *what could be*.

Organizing people to accomplish together what they would not or could not as individuals is a unique ability. It's also somewhat measurable, in terms of both process and outcomes. Thus, by focusing on this specific quality, we clarify what we mean by organizational leading and avoid confusing it with any number of qualities people call leadership, along with the emotional baggage of being and not being called a leader. Leaders who are not good at organizing others to accomplish what they would not or could not as individuals are ineffective, whether we call them leaders or not. They're not demonstrating the O Factor. When individuals are good at this, regardless of their position, title, or training, they are exhibiting the O Factor. By clarifying what it is that effective leaders really *do*, we untangle the knot that society has created over the last several decades.

While I can't speak for other cultures, as an American I'm very familiar with our concern that everyone be given a fair chance to succeed. There exists an almost paranoia about not recognizing some as more capable than others. Researchers Plomin and Caspi (1990) note, "Lurking in the shadows is the pervasive fear that genetic differences undermine the foundation of democracy. This confusion comes from thinking that to say that everyone is created equal is the same as saying that people do not differ genetically. The founding fathers of America were not so naïve as to think that all people are created identical. The essence of a democracy is that all people should have legal equality despite their genetic differences."[1]

So how does a child become an O Factor? Are they born that way or is it a matter of environment? That question is age-old, regardless of the talent type. All significant abilities are matters of both nature and nurture. In the old days, we thought of these as either/or, but now we realize they're both/and. A more effective question is, "What amount of an organizational leader's talent is nature (genetic) and what percent is nurtured (environmental)?" A simple matrix helps us think through this idea a bit further (see Graph 2.0).

A student with lower natural ability who's been raised in a strong leadership home and has been given opportunities to experience being in charge (lower right cell) will likely demonstrate some organizational skills. Opinions vary in terms of how far this person can progress. Students with average or below average organizational talent and no development (lower left cell) may be very intelligent and gifted in other areas, but will likely display few O Factor indicators. Re-creating environmental elements such as O Factor parents who model organizational skills, a family life that nurtures this kind of behavior, and friends who offer mentoring is very difficult. The typical alternative is periodic training events

	Low	Nurture	High
High	Gifted & Undeveloped (High capacity)		Gifted & Talented (Extreme capacity)
Nature			
	Normal & Undeveloped (Low capacity)		Normal But Trained (Moderate capacity)
Low			

Graph 2.0 Nature versus Nurture

offered by people who are not strong leaders themselves and/or programs that do not focus on executive skill development. Return on investment of nurturing lower organizational capacity students who are not naturally surrounded by developmental resources makes it difficult to justify at very young ages.

Students highly gifted in organizational ability who've not experienced much nurturing (upper left cell) will likely exhibit behaviors that reflect natural talent that's rough and underdeveloped. It would be similar to a natural athlete who's never played soccer being discovered by a talent agent or coach. The primary goal should be to figure out how we can identify upper left cell students and combine them with upper right cell members for accelerated project-based executive skill training, with individualized coaching and mentoring. We must offer intentional nurturing to those with the greatest potential to use it and catalyze their latent abilities. "People with a genetic inclination to lead, but no chance to act on that predisposition in childhood, are less likely to become leaders than those who have the same genetic tendency, but who also have the opportunity to try out leadership roles at school or in their families."[2]

The O Gene

At the time of publishing this book, no single genotype is known to cause the O Factor, but based on amazing breakthroughs in genome and neuroscience research since 2000, we understand a lot more about human nature and how people are wired. Recent discoveries in these fields make us think there is a "cocktail" of identified genes that significantly influence a child's inclination toward organizational influence. Even in 1972, the US Department of Education's Marland Report noted: "Various estimates of the proportions of intelligence variance due to heredity and environment, based on twin studies over a 20-year period, ascribe from 60 to 88 percent to heredity."[3] Although leadership ability research results are not as high, studies still denote a strong genetic predisposition for the O Factor. In his book "Born Entrepreneurs, Born Leaders," Dr. Scott Shane points out a variety of studies that estimate how much of characteristics related to leading are built into an individual's DNA. Depending on the study, 20-60% of an individual's inclination toward organizational skills can be attributed to genetic factors. These amounts and the context in which they're nurtured have a lot do with the observable talent.

Although this book is not focused on the behavioral genetic aspects of identifying O Factors, research helps us understand DNA-related elements that lean them in certain directions. To understand the gift of organizational leadership ability in students, we need to include a look at internal chemistry. Just as some are born to be tall, with brown eyes, heavier set, and hair that thins early, we inherit aspects of our wiring in the womb. Although organizational leadership is more than personality based, cognitive and temperament aspects directly impact an individual's ability to influence a group. Here are a few examples, based on scientific research in the field.

Intelligence and Leadership: Leadership emergence pertains to the perception of others that a person is "leader-like."

A common way of studying this is via groups without a designated leader, to see who emerges. Leadership effectiveness refers to more common research that measures how well people lead. Numerous studies since 1948 have shown that general intelligence is a relatively consistent predictor of leadership, in that those who emerge as leaders, or who are perceived to be leaders, possess above-average IQ. There appears to be about a 50% correlation between intelligence and leadership emergence.[4] As noted earlier in research on intelligence, a rather large percent (60-88) of IQ is determined to be hereditary. Intelligence among identical twins (sharing 100% of their genetic composition), raised separately, reveals an intelligence correlation of 75%.[5]

Although most research in the field of gifted and talented education focuses on the intellectually gifted, the Marland Report recognized that there isn't always a connection between IQ and other areas of gifting. "No distinction has been made between the academically, intellectually gifted and those who exhibit great prowess in the arts or who possess that quality of creativity one associates with the arts."[6] Although this is not as true for leadership ability, there are some similarities. Our work with student leaders globally reflects this informal observation. While leaders seem to be smart, they are often not smarter than everyone else. But those who are smarter often lack the social acumen required for effective organizational leading, such as the ability to read others and persuade them. This is what we respectfully refer to as "the geek factor," not necessarily social awkwardness, but just enough prowess deficiency to make them less effective in getting people to work together.

One example during our early work involved a young girl whose parents had PhDs. The participant seemed extremely intelligent and came up with brilliant ideas during the project-based training. The problem is that when it was her turn to be the Team Leader, she couldn't get her peers to buy into her ideas because of her ineffective social skills. At the end of the module, her mother said that she wouldn't be coming back. We asked, "Why?" The woman replied, "She just seems to have other interests." We didn't have the heart to tell her that she probably didn't find it fun because she couldn't get her team members to follow her, in spite of her obvious smarts.

Personality & Leadership Traits: All personality traits are not applicable to organizing others, but some are, specifically those related to helping people accomplish together what they would not or could not as individuals. Although the popularity of trait theories in the field of leadership studies ebbs and flows throughout the years, many who study them find a significant source is heredity. Kenny and Zaccaro (1983) found that 49-82% of the variance in leader emergence was attributed to characteristics of the leader, because these are the initial cues that others go on to determine who they will and will not follow.[7]

For example, one trait recognized and measured among leaders is social potency, the ability to persuade others to buy into your ideas and/or follow you. One study showed that 24% of the genetic effect on leadership comes from the same genes that affect social potency. The same genes that improve your ability to persuade will affect your likelihood of running project or planning events or leading things.[8] Scientists have found that roughly 40-50% of the differences in our personalities are linked to our genes, unrelated to family environment.[9]

Studies like these are often conducted on sets of twins. Identical twins (monozygotic) share the same DNA for the most part, because they emerged from a single fertilized egg as it divided. Fraternal twins (dizygotic) resulted from two separate fertilized eggs and only share the same amount of DNA as any other siblings, averaging around 50%, although it can vary widely, depending on the similarities and differences of the 50% that mom and dad donated. The twin registry database is very large and tracks siblings over many years, comparing those raised in similar environments with those separated at birth who lived in different homes. This research provides a foundation for understanding how much of the differences can be attributed to environment and how much to genetics.

"Shared environments do not appear to be a significant factor in influencing leadership. These results are consistent with research in other areas of behavioral genetics."[10] Another interesting factor is that "shared environments such as socio-economic status and common educations experiences (e.g. same grade and high school, etc.) don't seem to matter."[11] One recent study compared leadership behavior and personality characteristics, discovering that genes account for roughly 30% of the differences between people in terms of having a track record of leadership.[12]

Another study of twins raised in different families showed that 49% of the difference is genetic. Identical twins raised by different parents had the same leadership potential, 47% of the time, while fraternal twins raised together were the same in only 19% of the cases.[13] In a regression analysis of what predicted leadership emergence better, personality traits (i.e. Big Five) were found to be stronger than intelligence.[14]

Leadership Style: The natural tendency to organize others to accomplish isn't the only thing influenced by our inner chemistry. How we do it is as well. Two primary styles studied by leadership experts are called transactional and transformational. The former has more to do with positional authority and organizational decisions based on exchanging resources, services, and extrinsic reward. The latter focuses on inspiration, vision, charisma, and motivating people intrinsically by stimulating a higher sense of purpose. Research shows that genetic factors influence what type of organizational leadership style a person will adopt.[15]

Not Leading: Although we tend to look for attributes that incline people to lead and seek roles of organizational dominance, the inverse is true as well. Personality dimensions sometimes hinder people from becoming leaders, increasing the odds they won't take charge. These also involve a genetic factor. For example, neuroticism, a tendency to feel anxious and depressed, reduces our chances of being a leader, yet these feelings are known to have a genetic component to them.[16] Genes influence our temperaments. Transformational leaders purvey hope and inspire people to follow their vision. Some of this is because of their ability to focus on the potential good. They're optimists. People with more positive personalities attract people to follow them. Half of the difference in optimism or pessimism is genetic in nature.[17]

As we noted, about 50% of the Big Five personality factors are inherited (open to new experiences, conscientiousness, extroversion, agreeable, and neuroticism). Effective leaders tend to be higher on openness, conscientiousness (sense of responsibility), and extroversion and lower in agreeableness and neuroticism than others. One surprise for many is the agreeableness level, but being lower in this quality allows O Factors to make unpopular decisions when necessary, because they're likely to base decisions on the desire to be liked and keep peace. Thus, if your genetic wiring affects the level of these traits, your propensity to lead effectively (not to mention enjoy it) will be thwarted.

Science Pushing on Culture

The goal of this chapter is not to oversell the notion that people are hardwired to lead and that our success in life is based on genetic fate, but rather to push back on the cultural notion that you can be whatever you want to be. "We like to think that leadership—the ability to influence other people to work toward the achievement of a goal—is something anyone can learn. In fact, we want to believe that everyone is equally likely to be a leader.

The only difference between who takes charge and who doesn't, we tend to think, is how much people work for it. But that's not true. Whether you become a leader or not isn't simply a choice that you make. And it isn't just the result of how your parents raised you or what you learned in school. It comes, at least in part, from what you were born with, your DNA."[18] Just as centuries ago we pushed back on those who thought the world was round or that the sun was the center of the solar system, it's time for us to embrace the fact that a significant part of what makes up those talented at organizing is nested in their brain chemistry.

I enjoy looking at art. When you stare closely at an oil painting, you can see the individual dabs of paint. But as you back up, the painting comes alive as the various colors blend together and you see the still life, portrait, or landscape. When you look closely at those who lead, you can see these individual elements that seem to stand alone. But as you step back, you see how these elements make up the entire picture of the way an individual uses them to help others achieve together what they would not or could not as individuals. One of the newest fields of study is social neuroscience, the process of analyzing how the brain's chemistry and wiring affect social behaviors. In years to come, research in this area may discover interesting ways genetics impact O Factors' ability to organize and lead others.

Dr. Shane writes, "Much of the time that we think people are *learning* to become leaders they really aren't. People who are born with the versions of genes that increase their odds of becoming the boss are just more likely to find themselves in leadership-rich situations as they respond to their genetic predispositions"[19] I talked to him about why, in spite of the scientific research, so many people resist the idea that some people, including children and youth, demonstrate a predisposition to organize others and an ability to learn executive skills faster and better. His response intrigued me. He said that people don't have difficulty understanding physical genetics, as when you're able to measure the finger length of a pianist or flat webbed feet in an Olympic swimmer or arm span and vertical jump of a basketball player. But because things such as charisma and persuasion and organizational thinking are more internal, people become skeptical of what they can't see. Therefore, they doubt the viability that things other than physical qualities could be hereditary and thus assume we're all created equal in those areas. This reflects a philosophical mindset as opposed to a scientifically deduced conclusion.

Nature & Nurture

While genotype typically refers to our genetic wiring, phenotype is a term that encapsulates our observable self. It's a culmination of who we are, based on our genes and the environmental influences that helped shape us. The latter includes any number of externals, including parenting, education, cultural traditions, traumatic, home, and life experiences. This combination of influences makes us who we are.

People tend to enjoy what they're good at and receive affirmation from others, so you can see how a person's genetic gifting often leads to reinforcement from the environment. For example, a father notices his 2-year-old throwing balls with amazing accuracy and speed, unlike his peers. The parent begins paying special attention to this and starts playing catch regularly after work. A few years later he gets his boy into t-ball and then Little League, along with recruiting a local coach for private pitching lessons. The young child excels, gaining attention from others and being recruited by more competitive travel teams. So while you can't deny the role and importance of years of training and nurturing, much of this resulted from the natural ability evident in the preschooler. Growing up in cold country, I learned early that to build a good snowman, you had to begin with a good snowball. You'd roll the tight ball in the snow until it got big.

Genetics and environment create complex interactions. Even when we say that 45% of a specific organizational leadership quality is genetic, it doesn't mean that 55% is environmental, because how the latter engages the former produces variances. For example, typical research assumes that two children raised in the same home will share very similar experiences. But if one child has a genetic predisposition to being opinionated, strong willed, and taking risks, parents may push back on this child much harder than a more compliant, fearful sibling. Thus, because of the genetic differences between the children, parental responses may differ significantly. "Children with different genetic predispositions no doubt react differently to the same parent input, depending either on what they attend to, how they interpret their parents' actions, or what behavioral predisposition of their own has been triggered."[20] Even though they're in the same home with the same parents, their environmental influence will be quite different. This type of covariance complicates understanding the source.

Still, our chemical makeup draws us toward certain activities, piquing our interest that in turn gets reinforced when we're good at it. "Our genes influence our attitudes toward leadership, our leadership abilities, our willingness to adopt leadership roles, and even the kinds of leaders we become."[21] Organizational psychologist Melvin Sorcher and organizational sociologist James Brant summarize this nature-nurture combo in their analysis of corporations and how they go about identifying leaders. In a Harvard Business Review article they state, "Our experience has led us to believe that much of leadership talent is hardwired in people before they reach their early or mid-twenties. That means, as far as leadership is concerned, people are reasonably complete packages by the time they arrive at the corporate doorstep. Their ability to lead has already been shaped by a multitude of factors and experiences that took root early in their lives. Some of these were within their control; many others were happenstance. We have followed individuals at many organizations as their careers progressed and have found a remarkable stability and consistency in virtually all aspects of their behavior over time. Simply put, people do not change very much once they enter the corporate world, and the changes that do occur are mainly a matter of consolidation of strengths—or a downward drift in behavior that needs improvement."[22]

Some people who study talented and successful people look at early skill development and training, implying that if every child received numerous lessons and years of practice, they could do whatever they wanted. Unfortunately, looking at nurturing elements alone is inadequate. What typically happens, among those who exhibit outstanding performance ability, is that an early indicator gets noticed and then cultivated.

The nature-nurture combination is both/and, not either/or. That is the main reason behind work at KidLead: to identify those most apt to learn the sophisticated social skills of organizational leadership in order recruit them early for concentrated development. The younger you go, the more important it is to focus on gifting, since life experience is very low. The gift is like a seed. Any farmer knows that the yield of the seed is determined by a variety of factors, including soil quality, sunlight, moisture, temperature, fertilizer, and weed control. Farming is a complicated process. Cultivating components are important for any significant talent development, but you need the seed. The argument that everyone has the same seed is what we don't see in the area of organizational leadership, in children, youth, or adults. The research doesn't support it. Therefore, we want to identify the O Factor seed early, not only to provide a head start, but also to maximize developmental windows that are lost if we wait too long. "Leadership is explicitly the result of the interaction between our genes and the situations in which we find ourselves. Our genes influence our attitudes toward leadership, our leadership abilities, our willingness to adopt leadership roles, and even the kinds of leaders we become."[23]

Leadership Ability Is a Terrible Thing to Waste

"A mind is a terrible thing to waste." That's the tagline from an ad campaign that the United Negro College Fund ran, designed to get young African Americans into college. The phrase still haunts many of us today. But leadership ability is also a terrible thing to waste. That is why we need to identify and develop O Factors. "Many scientists believe that people with innate tendencies toward leadership are more likely than other people to become leaders only if they experience the kind of events that trigger those predispositions to become active."[24] Unfortunately, if students with a gift for organizing others are overlooked, they may never discover their potential.

Dr. Tom Harrison's work in identifying those gifted in entrepreneurism made him realize that just because you possess a natural talent doesn't mean it will ever develop. He notes that genes function more like a recipe than a blueprint. If you put all the right ingredients into a cake batter but set the heat too low and/or leave it in the oven too long, the product won't be as hoped.[25] The US Department of Education's Marland Report echoes this concern. "Gifted and talented youth are a unique population, differing markedly from their age peers in abilities, talents, interests, and psychological maturity. They are the most versatile and complex of all human groups, possibly the most neglected of all groups with special educational needs. The resultant waste is tragic."[26]

Even while finishing up this book, I discovered other studies looking at how the endocrine systems and testosterone effect dominance and how medial prefrontal cortex influences how people assess risk, aspects directly related to leader behavior.[27] So while we wanted to drive a stake in the ground that an increasing amount of scientific research shows that O Factors possess a wiring that lends itself to exceptional potential organizational leading, the impetus of the rest of this book is how to identify and develop it. Latent potential is what we might call dormant potential. What we want to do is to wake it up. Our primary premise is that O Factors need to receive intentional, professionally designed, accelerated training, but the first step is in understanding who is able to embrace this curriculum at a young age and who will benefit the most from it.

In the next chapter, we'll offer a look at how to identify O Factors, so that we can develop them more appropriately, per their gifts and abilities. We'll also provide a unique angle at what distinguishes those who lead from others.

Endnotes:

1. Plomin, R. and Caspi, A. 1990. Behavioral genetics and personality. In Behavioral Genetics, 2nd ed. W. H. Freeman: New York, p. 269.

2. Ilies, R., Arvey, R., and Bouchard, T. 2006. Darwinism, behavioral genetics, and organizational behavior: A review and agenda for future research. *Journal of Organizational Behavior*, 27(2): 121-141.

3. Marland Report, p. 33.

4. Ilies, R, Gerhards, M.W., and Le, H. 2004. Individual differences in leadership emergence: Integrating meta-analytic findings and behaviors genetics estimates, *International Journal of Selection and Assessment* 12(3) 207-219, p. 217.

5. Bouchard, T.J. 1997. IQ similarity in twins reared apart: Findings and responses to critics. In R.J. Sternberg & E.L. Grigorenko (Eds), *Intelligence: heredity and environment* (pp. 126-160). New York: Cambridge University Press.

6. Marland Report, p. 35.

7. Kenny, D.A., and Zaccaro, S. J. 1983. An estimate of variance due to traits in leadership. *Journal of Applied Psychology*, 68. 678-685.

8. Arvey, R., Zhang, Z., Avolio, B., and Krueger, R. 2007. Developmental and genetic determinants of leadership role occupancy among women. Journal of Applied Psychology, 92(3): 693-706.

9. Loehlin, J., McCrae, R., Costa, P., and John, O. 1998. Heritabilities of common and measure-specific components of the big five personality factors. *Journal of Research in Personality*, 32(4): 431-453. Harrison, T. L. (2005). Instinct: Tapping your entrepreneurial DNA to succeed in business. New York: Warner Business Books. Plomin, R., DeFries, J.C., & McClearn, G.E. (1990). Behavioral genetics: A primer (2nd ed.). San Francisco: Freeman.

10. Shane, S. Born Entrepreneurs, Born Leaders, 2010. Oxford University Press: New York, p. 128.

11. Arvey, R.D., Rotundo, M., Johnson, W., Zhang, Z., and McGue, M. (2006). The determinants of leadership role occupancy: Genetic and personality factors. The *Leadership* Quarterly 17, pp. 1-20.

12. Arvey, R., Rotundo, M., Johnson, W., and McGue, M. The determinants of leadership: The role of genetic, personality, and cognitive factors. *Journal of Applied Psychology*. (In process.)

13. Bouchard, T., McGue, M., Hur, Y., and Horn, J. 1998. The heritability of attitudes: A study of twins, *Journal of Personality and Social Psychology,* 80(6): 845-860.

14. Ilies, R, Gerhards, M.W., and Le, H. (2004).

15. Arvey, et al, 2006. Johnson et al., A., Vernon, P., Harris, J., and Jang, K. 2004. A behavior genetic investigation of the relationship between leadership and personality. *Twin Research*, 7(1): 27-32.

16. Shane, 2010, p. 128.

17. Plomin, R. 1994. Genetics and Experience: The interplay between nature and nurture. Thousand Oaks, CA: Sage.

18. Shane, 2010, p. 122.

19. Ibid., p. 133.

20. Maccoby, E. E. 2000. Parenting and its effects on children: On reading and misreading behavior genetics. *Annual Reviews Psychology*, 200. 51:1-27.

21. Shane, 2010, p.135.

22. Sorcher, M. and Brant, J. 2002. Are you picking the right leaders? *Harvard Business Review*, p. 7.

23. Shane, 2010, p. 134, 135.

24. Ibid., p. 136.

25. Harrison, T. L. (2005)

26. Marland Report, p. 42.

27. Arvey, R. D., Wang, N., Song, Z., and Li, W. (2014) The biology of leadership. In Handbook of leadership and organizations (73-90). Oxford, UK: Oxford Press.

The O Factor

Chapter 4

How do we identify an O Factor?

Dangers in Failing to ID

Although DNA is involved in O Factor giftedness, we don't advocate doing genetic testing to determine whether or not students possess the right genes for the purpose of developing them. But selecting those most apt to benefit from accelerated skill training is strategic. Properly identifying O Factors is important. We need to recognize who has the capacity to learn organizational leadership at a young age. By overlooking them, we do them a disservice. The US Department of Education's Marland Report noted a number of challenges that O Factors face in being properly identified and developed (as well as other gifted students).

- *According to the testimony and experience of professionals and parents of gifted and talented, our educational system has been*

45

inconsistent in seeking the gifted and talented, finding them early in their lives and individualizing their education. Our education system mirrors society's ambivalence and inconsistency toward the gifted and talented. Special injustice has occurred through apathy toward certain minorities, although neglect of the gifted in this country is a universal and increasing problem.

- *Existing services to gifted and talented children and youth do not reach large and significant subpopulations (e.g., minorities and disadvantaged) and serve only a very small percentage of the gifted and talented elementary and secondary population generally.*

- *Differentiated education for the gifted and talented is presently perceived as a very low priority at Federal, State, and most local levels of government and educational administration.*

- *There is an enormous individual and social cost when talent among the Nation's children and youth goes undiscovered and undeveloped. These students cannot ordinarily excel without assistance.*

- *Gifted and talented children are, in fact, deprived and disadvantaged, and can suffer psychological damage and permanent impairment of their abilities to function well which is equal to or greater than the similar deprivation suffered by any other population with special needs served by the Office of Education.[1]*

O Factor Specialists Needed

Because Dr. Sidney P. Marland, Jr. and his team of experts went outside of the traditional educational focus on intellectual and academic fields by including leadership ability, I was intrigued about this Commissioner of Education. I talked to a former work colleague of mine, Kami Gilmour, who is Dr. Marland's granddaughter. I also interviewed her father, Sid Marland, III. Both offered intriguing stories of Dr. Marland's life, professionally and personally. In addition to being a Colonel in the Army during World War II, he was a classroom teacher, school superintendent, and then US Commissioner of Education. The variety of his leadership roles and the opportunity to observe talented leaders made him recognize that academics alone do not improve society. Kami said that during family reunions, her grandfather wasn't a fan of small talk, but they often discussed politics, educational processes, and leadership.

In addition, organizational leadership played a big part of Dr. Marland's family ancestry. His grandfather owned and managed the largest brickyard in England. His father owned and managed a clothing store and led numerous philanthropic and fraternal groups in Connecticut. Sidney's two brothers, decorated WWII officers, became the Director of Public Health in Hawaii and a railway commissioner and radio station owner, respectively. As the old adage goes, "It takes one to know one." As someone with organizational acumen, Marland identified this ability in others, along with its importance.

As we mentioned previously, the Marland Report states, "Gifted and talented children are those *identified by professionally qualified persons* who by virtue of outstanding abilities, are capable of high performance" (italics added).[2]   What does it mean to be "professionally qualified" when it comes to organizational leadership? Educators, who specialize in academics and pedagogy, are apt to recognize intellectual ability. But specialists in organizational leadership should be the ones who develop the assessments and guidelines for identifying O Factors. Gaining knowledge in a specific field is a fundamental belief in education. This is not intended as a put-down of educators, since no one can specialize in everything. When you get the symptoms of a cold or flu, you may go to a general practice, family doctor. But if that physician notices something else, she'll likely recommend a specialist for further testing and diagnosis. Although educators see students in social settings and thus are most apt to observe organizational talent indicators, they should recommend further assessment and diagnosing from specialists in the field of organizational leadership and/or assessments created by them.

Looking at the Right Qualities

Identifying the right qualities in the selection of leaders is difficult at all ages. Sorcher and Brant (2002), in a Harvard Business Review article, noted how often companies hire and promote people who appear to have leader qualities, but who can't really lead. For example, often "superior problem-solving capabilities can mask a deficiency in long-range, conceptual, or strategic thinking. Being able to solve a problem is one thing; knowing which problem to solve—and then taking the initiative to solve it—is quite another."[3] They go on to say that many companies focus their resources on developing leaders rather than on accurately identifying them initially.

The Marland Report noted, "Many young (GT) people go unnoticed. Very little identification has been carried on in depth, or with proper testing instruments. Many of the assumptions about giftedness and its incidence in various parts of American society are based on inadequate data, partial information, and group tests of limited value."[4] Although the report was talking about GT students in general, this is certainly the case with current assessments designed to identify leadership ability in students. What are the qualities that help us identify students with the O Factor?

Most of the research on leadership has focused on two areas, emergence and effectiveness. Leadership emergence looks at how individuals step up to organize groups and how people select who they think is a leader and why they follow. The latter often involves implicit leadership, the sort of mental picture people have in terms of what a leader should do, be like, and at times even look like. For example, if you ask a group to do a task without designating someone to be in charge, who emerges as the organizer? While this is related to identifying O Factors, it is different in that our goal is to measure who demonstrates exceptional ability to learn organizational skills at a young age.

When you look at leader emergence, you need to make sure that you're focusing on the qualities that actually cause an individual to organize the group to accomplish a task together, not just who gives the impression of being a leader and/or who others think is a leader. Again, the challenge of this is not just in the area of children and youth. It's a common problem among adults, many of whom are sophisticated at hiring and organizational processes.[5]

Leadership effectiveness focuses on what makes organizational leaders good at what they do. Usually, the purpose of these studies is to learn how to get better. Hundreds of adult leadership assessments exist, but practically none are specifically designed to identify leadership potential. Nearly all were created to help organizational people improve their skills. Identification of organizational aptitude at a young age is different from leadership effectiveness.

Nearly all of the assessments used to identify leadership ability giftedness in students confuse qualities we seek in leaders with what distinguishes those who lead from non-leaders. For example, most would agree that leaders should be good listeners, because hearing out team members harvests ideas, improves trust, and engenders commitment. But good listening is also a skill that we value in all people, not just those who lead. Therefore, listening does not distinguish what leaders do from non-leaders. Conversely, the ability to convene people to work on a shared goal is something that distinguishes leaders from non-leaders. The former characteristic (listening) is what we may call a Type II quality, something we want our leaders to have, but doesn't specifically distinguish what leaders do uniquely from others. The latter quality (convening) is a Type I characteristic, something that leaders typically possess that differentiates them from others (see Graphic 3.0). In this model, Type III qualities would refer to those not pertinent to the leadership process (i.e. health, art, math &

kinesthetic skills), so we won't discuss those.

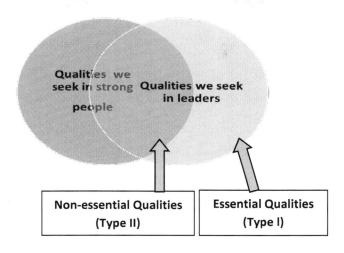

Graphic 3.0: Leader Qualities Types

If you review GT assessments with questions designed to identify leadership gifting, you'll notice that 80-100% cover Type II qualities. If you're offering a 360-assessment on a leader to target areas for improvement, these types of questions make more sense. Frequently, "What do you like most in a leader?" surveys prompt researchers to look at the qualities people desire in their bosses as opposed to what actually makes leadership happen. Type II characteristics can improve leader efficacy, but they're secondary. Identification of giftedness is different from skill improvement. If you're trying to qualify children or youth with a distinct talent for organizational leading, then Type II questions don't significantly aid in that process, because any number of students not gifted in leadership could do relatively well on them. When those who specialize in education and not organizational leadership create assessment questions, you're more apt to get items that lack clarity, in the same way leadership experts would not be strong in developing pedagogical surveys.

While we're on the subject of GT assessments that claim to identify leadership ability, let's point out two other common weaknesses in current instruments available. Some of these assessments measure a variety of talents and only focus a few questions on leadership (4-10 items), creating a very shallow look at the gift. Given that 80-100% of these are Type II questions, such a small sampling is even less likely to reliably identify leadership ability. Such instruments can offer basic pretests to see if more involved testing is warranted, but they should not be used to determine if the O Factor is present.

Some of the assessments also use self-responses, where students answer questions based on their own self-perceptions. The weakness of this is that adolescence is a period when we're grappling with our self-identify as well as social pressures for acceptance. To rely on feedback from people who are trying to figure out how others are reacting to their influence is unreliable. Plus, students with little to no formal leadership feedback are apt to find concepts related to organizational leadership challenging to understand, as even adults wrestle with it. A more reliable method is to use observers who've seen students in social settings, measuring their quality by the number and types of environments where they've seen the student.

SIS and NYLI Assessments

Our work the last several years in developing and implementing the Social Influence Survey (SIS), a 25-multiple choice question assessment completed by an adult on a student, offers a somewhat holistic approach to estimating organizational leadership aptitude (available free, online at www.kidlead.com). Answers are based on a 1- to 5-Likert scale, customized for each question. A consistent 6th answer option is "Unsure," providing low-level rater confidence qualification. Used by LeadYoung certified curricula trainers, the SIS offers a pragmatic approach in hopes of inviting students scoring over 3.60 into a project-based training program. We collected data from over 4000 assessments on nearly 3000 students, over the course of 7 years.

We are in the process of scientifically testing a more robust instrument, called the Nelson Young Leader Inventory (NYLI), consisting of 32-multiple choice questions. This includes a more involved rater survey to measure the quality of responders' answers. All of the items involve interpersonal outcomes, loosely divided into 4 categories (Table 1.0). The goal of NYLI is to focus on Type I leader qualities (causal) and avoid Type II (correlational), creating a more refined assessment for identifying organizational leadership gifting.

By focusing on the essential qualities required for leading, you avoid two common errors—false positives and confusing correlation with cause-and-effect. When too many Type II qualities are used in inventories, you often identify students with charming personalities, who are likable and have people skills, but when asked to organize others, can't. This is common in student governments, where candidates get voted in by peers, based on looks, likeability, charisma, and familiarity. Although these qualities are common among effective leaders, they are not essential for leading. Thus, when you ask an associated student body (ASB) council to plan a big event, half of the members develop a glazed stare, akin to the spinning circle on your computer when it's trying to reboot or locate a software program.

So while we frequently see a number of Type II characteristics evident in effective leaders whom we like and admire, many of these would also be evident in highly functioning, self-actualized individuals who were ineffective leaders. Can these qualities help a leader be more effective? They can, which is why they are often included in 360-improvement instruments, but these items don't *cause* leadership. They are also evident in people who do not lead.

Type I Leader Qualities (NYLI)	Type II Leader Qualities

<ul><li>P1. Persuasive: the ability to get others to see things differently and buy into your ideas and vision; a.k.a. social potency</li><li>P2. Propelled: internal *locus of control*, efficacy, achievement-oriented, inspiring others to persevere</li><li>P3. Planner: comfortable with abstract thinking, can come up with ideas and assign tasks that others accept</li><li>P4. Power: exudes boldness, courage and confidence that impresses others to notice and follow</li></ul>	<ul><li>21st Century Skills:
	   * Critical thinker / decisive
	   * Collaborative / relational
	   * Creative / curious
	   * Communicates / listens</li><li>Confident / high self-esteem</li><li>Humble / open-minded</li><li>Moral / ethical</li><li>Positive / hopeful</li><li>Charismatic / likeable</li><li>Smart / intelligent</li><li>Flexible / adaptable</li></ul>

Table 1.0 Type I (Essential) and Examples of Type II (Non-essential) Leader Qualities

This is why in adult organizational life, we often recruit, promote, and hire individuals who appear to be leaders we've seen in the past, but fail miserably because they do not possess the O Factor, the essentials required to catalyze leadership. Just because a person is smart, relational, charismatic, and ethical or has occupied a position of supervision in the past, doesn't mean s/he can lead. Many of the characteristics correlate with good leading, but they don't cause the effect we seek, creating frustration for everyone and making us wonder what went wrong in the process. By gathering appropriate feedback from 2-3 raters who've observed a student in social settings, you can identify those with a strong probability of being an O Factor. Initial recommendations could come from people such as teachers, coaches, parents, and child/youth workers.

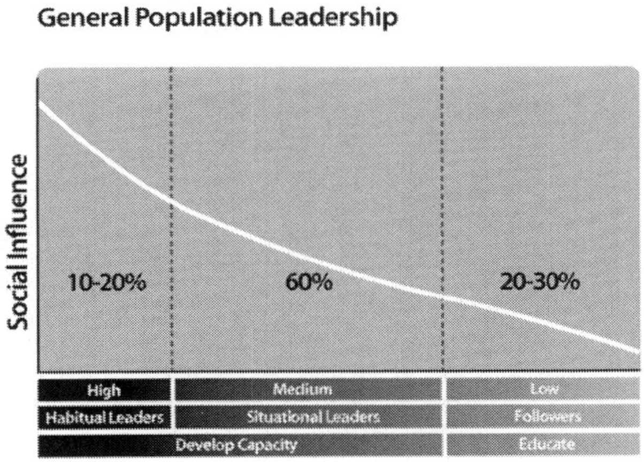

General Population Leadership

Graph 4.0   Organizational Leadership Aptitude Categories

In Graph 4.0, three categories are illustrated, with results similar to a normal distribution curve. The left one is what we refer to as Habitual Leaders. These students are high in social influence and seek situations where they can lead and get energized by organizing others. Sometimes they try to take over where they shouldn't, but it is a natural, intuitive process for them, even if they lack experience and exhibit some rough edges. The Marland Report suggests that most GT students place among the top 3-5%, although it also recognizes that these amounts may vary. We suggest development within the 10%, noting that it's better to think more broadly than narrowly and see how potential O Factors do in more concentrated training opportunities. Plus, since leadership capacity is often under-developed among the very young, we recommend at least considering those identified within this category. The extension to 20% is designed to focus on those who may come from under-identified populations (i.e. poor, certain ethnic cultures valuing collectivism and compliance among the young). This category needs intentional, accelerated training to hone their skills and develop their latent potential. That has been our primary focus the last decade.

The middle section, Situational Leaders, includes those who can learn to lead in certain contexts. Members in this category are more apt to benefit from training as adults, after they've matured socially-emotionally and gained sufficient life experience that can be translated into organizational management at various levels. Many of these people emerge as middle managers, small business owners, teachers, and project leaders. Organizational leading tends to deplete their energy. The idea that burnout comes from overwork is misleading. Burnout is a result of spending too much of our time in areas where we're not gifted or passionate. Laboring within our strengths actually energizes us. I'm not overly concerned about this broad middle section, because while they may emerge in organization leadership roles later in life, they're not apt to be your top leaders and we've not found them able to learn accelerated skills at a young age. By placing these middle section students into a concentrated organizational leadership training program, you'll intimidate them, frustrate higher octane organizers, and potentially diminish their confidence and self-identity. Developmental programs can come later as adults for this category.

The category on the right represents students who may be extremely talented and intelligent but do not enjoy (and would be dealt a disservice) if asked to organize others. Being in charge could eat away at their self-esteem. This group should be empowered to use their talents and resources in supportive roles. More appropriate organizational goals involve educating them on leadership as a social process and helping them learn team skills, not focusing on leading.

Although the NYLI will be available soon, the SIS can be used now to estimate organizational leadership aptitude. It is based on a combination of teacher surveys, a synthesis of adult leadership assessments, and is adjusted from feedback received from its use on 1000s students in various countries and cultures. The SIS is free, online, at www.kidlead.com. Adults take the assessment on students. Those who push the "Parent" button receive processed feedback on the student. Following is a list of categories suggesting the likelihood of organizational giftedness, based on our assessment and observations of 6- to 18-year-olds the last 10 years.

SIS Scores:

- 1.00-2.49 Very low probability of leadership giftedness
- 2.50-3.00 Low probability of leadership giftedness
- 3.01-3.49 Slight probability of leadership giftedness
- 3.50-3.79 Modest probability of leadership giftedness
- 3.80-4.39 High probability of leadership giftedness
- 4.40-5.00 Very high probability of leadership giftedness

Again, these figures will vary slightly, depending on age, socio-economic demographics, and cultural influence in regard to adult-child social norms and familial customs, as well as the quality of the rater's observations.

Multiple Assessments

Experts in the GT field suggest multiple assessment strategies, as opposed to relying on a single instrument. While the SIS and NYLI may be the strongest tools available, a suite of tools may offer a more robust process in identifying O Factor abilities justifying concentrated development.

- *Current GT assessments:* As mentioned, you could use other GT instruments that claim to measure leadership ability, even if they focus on Type II characteristics instead of Type I, so long as they were limited to pre-tests. This could include adult responders and self-assessments.

- *Peer ratings:* In addition to adult surveys, you might augment these with peers rating those who they respect as group organizers, so long as the questions reflect O Factor characteristics. "Who would you want to be put in charge of class if the teacher stepped out?" "Who would you select as a team captain?" "Who have you seen step up as a group leader in the past?" Because the O Factor is a social function, getting input from a variety of others can be a productive way to see who is perceived to be more naturally influential.

- *Teacher/coach/parent recommendations:* Adults who have observed a student in social settings may offer good recommendations, especially if they've been given a basic understanding of what kind of social and organizational behaviors to note. We recommend this as a first step, followed by the SIS/NYLI.

- *Project-based observations:* Because the O Factor is primarily a social skill, you can invite students to participate in project-based activities and see how they respond when given the role as project manager and/or where no one person is deemed team leader, to see who rises to the occasion. With some basic rater training, adults can provide real-time observation and share qualitative feedback on what they see. (For more info on these, please contact us through our website: www.kidlead.com.)

Open Mindedness

Even though classroom teachers and educators are the

most apt to see O Factor indicators, because of their involvement in student socializing, there is often an adversarial attitude toward O Factors. The Marland Report noted, "Identification of the gifted is hampered not only by costs of appropriate testing—when these methods are known and adopted—but also by apathy and even hostility among teachers, administrators, guidance counselors and psychologists."[6] The report also noted that recognizing any students as gifted and talented, let alone those with leadership ability, seems to be an uphill battle. "Only 3% of the experts felt that pupil personnel workers show a positive attitude toward the gifted, while 22% of the responses described negative attitudes, other concerns, or apathy and indifference toward the gifted. Studies have shown that pupil personnel workers are indifferent or hostile in their attitudes toward the gifted, it is supported as well by the general failure to seek and recognize the gifted in the schools."[7]

Ultimately, the onus of responsibility for identifying O Factors will likely come down to forward-thinking educators and in-tune parents. Few are as motivated to assist children and youth than parents. The influence of an informed parent can go a long way in the life of a child as well as within a school and educational system.

In the next chapter, we'll look at the most common indicators of the O Factor, so you can begin noticing who these children and youth are as you observe them in social settings.

Endnotes:

1. Marland Report (1972), US Department of Education: Washington DC, (114-115).

2. Ibid. p. 20

3. Sorcher, M. and Brant, J. Are you picking the right leaders. Harvard Business Review, Feb., 2002.

4. Marland Report (p. 114)

5. Sorcher and Brant (2002).

6. Marland Report (p. 10)

7. Ibid. p. 62

Chapter 5

What are leading O Factor indicators?

There are leaders, and there are those who lead. The former are people who occupy positions of authority, charged to oversee projects and programs. The latter are individuals who inspire others to accomplish together what they would not or could not as individuals. So who are those who lead? How can you identify them as children and youth?

Following are 10 behavioral indicators that convey the likelihood of leadership ability giftedness. They are among the most readily observable and often stand out among the others. They represent a synthesis of social behaviors noted in the SIS assessment that was developed using an array of methods, including teacher surveys on describing classroom influencers, a synthesis of dozens of adult leadership assessments, and nearly a decade of observing 1000s of preteens and teens from a variety of nations and cultures. They've also been modified and confirmed by over 200 adults trained to recognize organizational leadership social behaviors among 10- to 18-year-olds. This list is designed as a practical means for recognizing potential O Factors without completing an assessment. Even though all 10 are not what we'd deem essential characteristics for organizational leading, this starter set allows you to pre-qualify children and youth for a more robust analysis.

10 Leading Indicators

1. Peers listen to the student when s/he talks.

Even if everyone is talking, only a few are listened to and taken seriously. Years ago, an investment firm ran an ad campaign stating, "When E.F. Hutton talks, people listen." Some refer to this as the E.F. Hutton effect. Regardless of being an introvert or extrovert, O Factors are the ones taken more seriously. Don't confuse talkers with influencers. The length of time a person talks is not as important as the weight of what he says. Sadly, many students get overlooked in social settings. While they can benefit from assertiveness training and speaking skills, being comfortable communicating is still different from being heard and heeded. O Factor students get their message across, no matter how eloquent their public speaking. Watch the student in a social setting and observe how others respond to her while she speaks. Observe others' body language as they respond to the student. How many turn their heads and angle of their bodies toward them? These are symptoms of this indicator. Generally, O Factors not only gain the attention of peers, they also are listened to by adults.

2. Peers seek the student's opinion, asking what s/he wants to do, and then peers follow.

I grew up in a farming community in southwest Iowa, attending a small country school. At recess, my classmates asked me what we were going to play. Sometimes I'd pick soccer or softball, and other times it would be dodge ball or Red Rover. I also remember parent-teacher conferences, after which my parents scolded me, saying that the teacher didn't like me being a class clown. As I look back, I realize it was primarily because I stole classmates' attention. My budding influence abilities were not appreciated in school and were actually punished. The same is true of many O Factor students.

The difference between this indicator and the previous one is that if the O Factor student is not present or has not shared his opinion, peers seek him out to discover what he thinks. Whether it's knowing what to play at recess or getting a perspective on clothing, a video game, movie or song, O Factors are sought out by others. The same is true among adults. You can tell the natural leaders because you hear their names mentioned in social circles and during staff and board meetings. Children and youth have their own mini-cultures where a minority influences the majority. The difference between social niceties, being polite and listening to others, is that O Factors tend to be followed. O Factors are noticed when they are absent or haven't checked in on a subject. "Where's Abigail today?" "I haven't seen Michael." Even in their silence, O Factors convey influence.

3. The student initiates projects, seems ambitious, and challenges status quo in a way that engages others.

Most O Factors are achievement-oriented, dissatisfied with long periods of playing video games, watching television, and sitting around. They tend to be active. They get excited about projects. They exhibit a healthy curiosity related to their interests. They neither wait for parents or peers to give them goals, nor do they take the path of least resistance. Sometimes we're asked if this quality is confused with attention deficit disorder (AD/HD). This is the most diagnosed behavior disorder among school-aged children (3-5%). Although I've met several adult O Factors who claim to have attention deficit disorder, the big difference between a normal student with AD/HD and an O Factor is whether or not others follow them. You'll hear this distinction throughout this book because that is the essence of organizational influence and is what differentiates behaviors done by individuals without influence from behaviors displayed by those who lead organizations.

O Factors possess a sense of self-efficacy, an achievement-oriented attitude that propels them, causing them to push through barriers and inspire others to do that same. This indicator is related to an internal locus of control, the sense that you are in charge of your destiny and can obtain goals, in spite of circumstances and challenges.

4. The student gets accused of being bossy or seems highly opinionated by others, yet peers pay attention to them.

Right or wrong, O Factors tend to have a lot of ideas about things. They are usually willing to share these when asked and sometimes when they're not. They like to take charge and have others implement their ideas. When this happens, girls get accused of being bossy more than boys, who tend to be labeled as confident. The same is true in research regarding women and men leaders. This norm, common in most cultures, does an injustice to women leaders, because of the labeling and misunderstanding and subsequent misperceptions and responses. Opinionated and bossy students are also typically strong-willed. A child can be strong-willed and not an organizational leader, but many O Factors are.

If your child is not bossy or strong-willed, it doesn't mean that s/he lacks organizational aptitude. Perhaps she has learned when to give her opinions and is emotionally mature enough to recognize when she should and should not act out, especially when adults are involved. Therefore, an absence of this quality does not necessarily indicate a lack of aptitude, but the presence of this quality often is a sign. This characteristic benefits from intentional training so that an O Factor learns to not offend others and succeed in organizing when adults are in charge, by influencing superiors with more power.

One other exception of this indicator is that it tends to be more of a Western social behavior. Our work in Southeast Asia has taught us that most Asian students would not respond this way to an adult authority figure (teacher, parent), as this would be perceived as disrespectful and rebellious. At the same time, parents would not likely acknowledge this on a survey, even if it was evident.

5. The student gets selected as class monitor, team captain, or group leader by adults.

I teach non-leader-oriented adults that one way to determine if a new person has leadership ability is to interview her, listening for influence roles in her past. Adults often intuitively spot O Factors in class, religious school, and the ball field, and give them official roles of authority. They frequently do this unconsciously, to gain the respect of the young organizer and tap into her natural ability to control her peers. It eases teaching and coaching by decreasing disruptions. Leaving the class under the eye of a student influencer or putting the captain in charge of team calisthenics lightens the burden of the adult.

Adult O Factors often reflect this pattern. They refer to being recognized for their potential and are picked to run for an office, be captain of a project team, or manage groups in a company. Those most trusted for direction setting are often selected for roles of influence. Yet you don't have to wait until adulthood to observe consistencies in this type of social selection. A brief interview can offer great insights about others choosing the student to run for an organizational leadership role.

An exception is if a student is perceived to be a negative distraction and if a teacher has not earned the respect of the O Factor, they will not be selected because of their influence. The authority figure is concerned the student will organize peers away from positive behavior or desired goals and does not trust them. In this case, they are intentionally overlooked for authority roles because of their influence, combined with a perceived lack of character and self-discipline.

Also note this is about adults selecting students. As we mention in this book, frequently youth who get elected by peers for organizational roles such as student government, confuse looks and likeability for organizational skills. When students select peers for associated student body roles, there's a 50/50 chance you won't get an O Factor. When adults nominate influential students, the percent increases that you will.

6. **The student has been disciplined for being a distraction in class or on a team.**

As we just mentioned, sometimes O Factors get pegged as trouble makers or at least called out for organizing peers away from the desired goals of adults in charge. My wife, Nancy, remembers being pulled aside and confronted by her youth pastor during a church outing. She said, "Everyone's goofing around. Why did you pick on me?"

"Because, you're a leader," he responded.

"I don't want to be a leader," she answered.

"It doesn't matter. You are," he explained.

Teaching is hard work, at least teaching well is. When a teacher is not skilled in identifying and developing O Factors, s/he often feels competition with a student possessing organizational aptitude. Later in this book, we offer a chapter providing teachers practical ways to develop O Factors in their classroom and another on how to tap their influence for the benefit of the school. But when there's one teacher to 15, 20, or even 30 or more students, compliance is valued. If 5-10% of any given class is wired to organize others, these students will gain attention naturally. When a budding O Factor exudes a sense of humor, tells jokes, or makes snide remarks, classmates transfer their attention away from the teacher or assignment. The young influencer is deemed a class disrupter and troublemaker.

Non-compliant but non-organizer students are far less problematic, because they are primarily seen as irritating by their classmates and do not threaten class control. As a result, O Factors often receive more negative attention for inappropriate comments or distracting actions because they post a greater threat to an adult trying to maintain attention and control. Principals see future CEOs and entrepreneurs in their offices weekly.

7. The student negotiates well with peers and adults.

Let's say that your 11-year-old, Talea, has a 9:00p.m. bed time on school days, but tonight she's engrossed in a Disney movie. "Oh Mom, c'mon. My homework is done, and I'm ready for school tomorrow. Why can't I stay up until 10?"

"Because, honey, you know how rushed it gets in the morning," Mom defends. "Nine is your bedtime."

"But, Mom, this is a really good movie," Talea responds. "What if I lay out my clothes, make my lunch, and get everything ready during the commercials?"

"I don't know," Mom stammers. "I don't want you groggy in class."

"It's just an hour," Talea explains. "Besides, I'll help you get sissy ready if you want."

Mom pauses. "Well, okay, but no later than 10."

What happened? Mom was set on having her daughter in bed at 9, but Talea pleaded a strong case for staying up later. Scenarios like these are quite common with O Factors. They are able to articulate their ideas and present them in such a way that persuades both peers and adults. You'll hear people comment, "Someday, you're going to be a lawyer." They recognize the child's negotiating skills but are also implying that leading is an adult behavior, not a young person's. Young O Factors typically don't throw fits to get their ways, because they understand the art of persuasion. They may wear down adults, who eventually put a stop to the negotiating or just give in, but they're naturally good at selling others on their ideas.

Just as we noted that bossy-ness is more common in Western cultures, the ability to negotiate well is more common in Asian cultures. Let's say a teen wants to get his peers to go to the mall. An O Factor will bring up the idea and softly but intentionally persist in discussing the fun, the benefits, and the opportunities, until his peers eventually comply. While stealthier in nature, the teen demonstrated his ability to organize others toward a common goal that he preferred.

8. The student is good at organizing younger children and peers in activities or play.

While adults tend to rely on titles, organizational flow charts, and positional authority, students tend to be more organic in the way they influence. They are by nature more transformational in their style, which is also known to have a stronger genetic source than transactional leading. An early sign of organizational aptitude is a student's ability to gather younger children and peers in activities. Perhaps it's getting kids in the neighborhood to play house, or having them take turns on the trampoline, or doling out rules for a game they created. This is what behavioral psychologists refer to as social potency, the ability to persuade others to do something. When you see a pied piper in the neighborhood, chances are you're observing an O Factor. Although self-esteem and confidence issues can retard organizing among peers and older people, more reticent O Factors often display their influencing gifts among younger kids and preteens. This often makes them popular babysitters and childcare assistants. Take time to observe socializing patterns among students, where an adult authority figure is not present. You'll notice the organizers as they catalyze play, activities, and even roles among the members.

9. **The student stands up for his or her values and is more prone to create peer pressure than succumb to it.**

This is a good quality during adolescence, when self-centeredness morphs into social awareness and dreaded peer pressure. O Factors comply less when tempted by others, so long as the temptation goes against their basic beliefs. When high moral standards are missing, O Factors can persuade others to do things that are unethical, as can be seen in young gang leaders and neighborhood bullies. Compliant students are more vulnerable to the opinions of others and usually exhibit less organizational aptitude.

A weakness of this quality is that sometimes O Factors need to be taught tolerance of others, because they tend to avoid those who do not share their standard of ethics. Agreeableness is a personality quality that causes people to get along with others and be sensitive to their views. As we mentioned before, organizational leaders tend to be lower in agreeableness in that they don't need the support of others in making a difficult decision. But the downside of this is it can also make them less sensitive to those with differing opinions, causing them to write off others or avoid them altogether, which can work against us when we want to be effective with people.

In addition to standing up for their own values, O Factors feel a sense of responsibility for correcting injustices they see around them. They'll defend a friend or peer who is being taken advantage of or will push back on a rule that doesn't seem fair. This innate desire to correct injustices is what makes an O Factor valuable, so long as s/he possesses high moral standards. When an O Factor does not, that same person will not comply with good standards and will become a rule breaker, corrupting others in the process.

10. The student seems to be liked by others, who in turn try to emulate and/or follow them.

When we surveyed public school teachers, one of the consistent attributes they noted about classroom organizers was their likeability. O Factors tend to be better groomed, take care of their looks, and are generally friendlier than most. This attention to appearance reveals an implicit social skill that O Factors understand about being effective with others. While we may be tempted to dismiss this impetus on externals, thinking this just happens among the young, research shows that adults exhibit a bias for those who keep up their physical appearance. We even tend to vote for taller political candidates, identify strength and beauty with influence, and lean toward following those who present themselves well.

Popularity can happen without organizational influence, but most O Factors tend to be better liked than others. The wallflower—the loner, introverted, and socially awkward student—is not followed. They can still influence in what they create as inventors, artists, and entrepreneurs, but it is a different influence than organizing. That is why we stress that LeadYoung training programs are not designed as a charm school or to mainstream the socially challenged. O Factors need a certain amount of emotional intelligence to be effective, which shows up in how they relate to others. Those who are good at relating to others possess the likeability factor. Again, you can be likeable and not organize, but O Factors are typically likeable, emulated, and followed.

What is interesting is that studies show that leadership qualities are often seen over time and across a variety of settings (domains). Adults who occupy roles of leadership frequently did so as youth. Dr. Richard Arvey and a team of researchers showed that leading is generalizable.[1] Adult leaders for the most part recognize leadership roles they held as adolescents. So while organizational leaders can blossom later in life, most provide indicators very early.

Cultural & Age Nuances

Our work in Thailand, Singapore, Peru, Dubai, and with people from other cultures around the world has taught us a lot about cultural nuances in terms of how people organize. What we've been so surprised by is how similar most cultures are in terms of the process. Thus, our definition of leadership, being the process of people accomplishing together what they would not or could not do alone, is very fitting. Sometimes the way people catalyze leadership, as females or young people, is different between cultures, but the process itself is far more similar than it is dissimilar.

One interesting thing we learned in working with preschoolers is that O Factors at this age often exhibit some behaviors you do not see in older children. For example, they seem to identify with adult authority figures and want to share in the limelight and power that teachers possess. Thus, they like being a "helper." A preteen who wants to help the teacher may be more of a follower than a leader, but not so among preschoolers. Very young O Factors also play fantasy games such as "school," "house," or "fireman." Those who initiate this type of role playing usually establish themselves as authority figures and recruit others into follower roles. You don't see that among older children as you do among the very young.

Identification Then Development

Someone said, "To identify without development is educational malpractice." Once we've figured out which students are more than likely O Factors, what do we need to do to develop them? That is the primary focus of my work this last decade, creating training curricula modeled after executive programs that offer project-based methods and Socratic coaching. Naturally, since most schools focus on intellectual development with some athletic and art offerings, concentrated organizational leadership skills training is all but missing from most educational institutions. Token nods are provided in class representatives and student government positions, but these rarely offer training, other than on-the-job event planning.

Although LeadYoung curricula are age-n-stage developmental training programs, the remainder of this book will look at an array of ways we can support O Factor development as well as avoiding things that thwart their growth. The final chapter will introduce the training curricula, but there are a large number of things we can do and prepare for in the way we interact with these gifted organizers.

Regardless of how you develop your O Factor students, it's not enough just to identify them so you can "keep your eye on them" in the future. We need to be offering opportunities for them to develop their gifts and talents, just as students gifted in other areas need to be challenged with unique and concentrated curricula. Public and private schools host the most significant social environment in a young person's life, yet most do little or nothing that reflects organizational leadership training. The least we can do is make sure we're not thwarting their development.

In the next chapter, we'll introduce some very practical ways that we can develop young O Factors, regardless of their age.

Endnote:

1. Arvey, R. D., Kyong, W. P., and Tong, Y. K. (2011). The generalizability of leadership across activity domains and time periods. *The Leadership Quarterly, 22,* 223-237.

Chapter 6

Why is the 10/13 Window so critical?

If you want to train leaders you have to start early, but it isn't easily done. We have to conduct research, educate a wider public, and mobilize citizen allies. We have to persuade diverse groups to work together – school, social agencies, the faith community, law enforcement, all levels of government and soon. - John W. Gardner (6th US Secretary of Health, Education, and Welfare)

Tender Sprouts

Planting crops in the Midwest (US) where I grew up can be precarious. If you begin too early, chances are a freeze will kill the fragile sprouts. If you begin too late, the crop won't mature sufficiently for harvest. The first hard freeze abruptly ends its development. There is a window when farmers must get the seed in the ground if they want to reap a great, not just a good, crop. The same is true of leadership. The prime window for O Factors to learn ethical organizational leadership is precariously positioned in four critical years, from ages 10 to 13. We call this the 10/13 Window. Most colleges and high schools have some type of leadership-oriented program, even if they don't specifically identify gifted leaders or train them with executive skills curricula. Some middle schools have such programs. But when we talk about concentrated training for 10- to 13-year-olds, people can't fathom this. The Center for Creative Leadership did a survey of 462 managerial leaders, asking them when leadership development should begin. Nearly all said it should begin by 21, 90% said by 18, but 50% said it should start by 10 years of age. [1] What that development looks like may be nebulous in their minds, but more today are acknowledging the need to begin early.

Although we typically don't think of organizational leadership at this age, we frequently recognize this stage as a place to begin with many other things. Not long ago, a news story noted that college football teams are beginning to look at middle school students with significant athletic ability and stand-outs in Pop Warner football teams. A noted coach in Southern California trains preteens, with parents standing in line to sign up their next NFL star. Competitive hockey leagues in Canada begin recruiting the most talented children by 6 years of age. Gifted and talented programs typically suggest age 10 for formal testing and identification of academic abilities. So while some may resist this "Tiger Mom" mindset of pushing a child too early, there is some science behind the idea of identifying and developing talent very early.

In the field of psychology and child development, the 10/13 Window is more commonly referred to as preadolescence or early adolescence. (Year 13 is sometimes considered adolescence, depending on the model.) Strong, virtuous character is vital for effective, ethical organizational leadership. History primarily consists of good leaders staying good, good leaders going bad, and evil leaders behaving badly. Outside of significant inventions (e.g., Guttenberg press, penicillin, airplane, computer) and disasters (e.g., bubonic plague, Mount Vesuvius, malaria, influenza), a majority of history centers on the rise and fall of civilizations at the hands of adventurers and political, civil rights, and military leaders.

Every week we hear new accounts regarding leaders gone wild, those who cook the books, shaft investors, and let their egos get in the way of good judgment. The masses suffer from the decisions of a few. That is the downside of leadership. Most of us have worked for at least one questionable leader who requires us to tiptoe through mine fields, eventually creating a debris field of hurting people and organizational chaos. You know the challenge of effective, ethical leading firsthand. For the most part, these failures find their roots in inadequate preparation during developmental windows, when character is molded.

Effective and ethical leading go hand in hand. You can't be effective and unethical, because eventually you reap what you sow. The person who lies, cheats, embezzles, manipulates, and abuses people on their way to the top eventually gets discovered, and all too often the organization that he built crumbles. What is true of companies is also true of countries. Look in the rearview mirror of organizational life and you'll see it's strewn with examples of unethical influencers who've crashed and burned, along with those who surrounded them. Some used to think the key to effectiveness was unethical leading and taking the shortcut to success, but over the long haul, good character makes good sense and cents. That's why we need to start early to develop character in the context of effective organizational skills.

Effective Leading Is Ethical Leading

Hybrid vehicles combine the technology of two energy sources, a combustion engine and an electric motor. When you're driving, you often cannot detect whether you're using gas or electricity as the vehicle switches back and forth between the two. This serves as a metaphor for ethical leadership. The goal is to develop leaders who are so grounded in good character that they don't hesitate when making ethical choices while leading. Their inner compass directs them toward true north, so they consistently make decisions that bring value to others and benefit society as a whole.

Even ethical leaders have to wrestle over decisions that create loss, regardless of the choice made. Do we lay off employees or reduce stockholders' profits? Do we cut a deal that is legal but goes against some of our organizational values, even though it would be profitable? Issues like these litter the daily schedules and sometimes the nighttime sleep of leaders around the world. But far too much wrestling takes place over issues that should be simple because the ethical components essential to good leading dictate it. High standards make leading easier in that we are less distracted by issues that should be clean cut, allowing us to tend to other important matters. Figuring out how to connive, cheat, deceive, and cover up are ultimately taxing.

Leader decisions are influenced by who leaders are as people and how they think in terms of values and standards. This relates to character. Therefore, we should all be concerned about the character of a leader and his or her internal compass. Some like to think who a leader is as a person has little to do with how s/he functions. Unfortunately, this is not the case over the long haul. Rarely will a leader take personal commitments lightly while taking corporate commitments seriously. If you go back on your word with your family, you're apt to do it with colleagues. If you cheat on the golf course, you're likely to cut corners in the boardroom. Ultimately, you cannot separate who you are as a person from how you operate as a leader. A leader's character unconsciously impacts his or her decision making.

Compartmentalizing is the process of separating our lives into a variety of non-overlapping areas. People separate their personal lives from their public lives when they use different standards on the job than they use at home. Compartmentalizing seems to work for some, but it rarely works for organizational leaders. While we can point to examples of leaders who seemed to cheat their way to the top or maintained a dark side with few consequences, these are extreme exceptions. Society craves leaders who naturally make ethical decisions.

Learning organizational leadership skills in the context of ethical behavior allows O Factors to discover how they go together. Organizational leading is about dealing in power, but power tends to gravitate toward the dark side of human nature. Most yearn for power, as it prevents what we fear most—powerlessness. But history is replete with examples of power ruining people. So how can we immunize future leaders from this disease? We need to inoculate them early. Just teaching morality alone isn't enough. We must show them how leading involves ethical decisions and what it means to treat people with honor when you're the boss. Integrity, humility, and honesty are girders in trustworthy organizing. We don't want leaders to detach ethics from organizational contexts, so we need to show them how they go together.

Return on Investment in the 10/13 Window

The 10/13 Window is important for O Factor development
because it lies in the intersection of several developmental
characteristics, unlike at any other stage. This short era in life is
like a roundabout where various roads converge. Let's look briefly
at three of the patriarchs of developmental psychology, who
codified stages of human development: Kohlberg, Piaget, and
Erikson.

Moral development: Even though Lawrence Kohlberg came after
Piaget, we focus on him first because of his work in the area moral
development, critical if we are to develop ethical leaders. Although
he built on the ideas of Piaget, his unique system explained moral
growth through three sequential levels, each possessing two stages
(six total). Kohlberg noted that most people never get past the
fourth stage, even as adults. The first level and its two stages
develop through age 9. But beginning at age 10, the Conventional
level begins. This is the level most adolescents and adults remain
in their entire lives (85%), explaining why some say that the person
you are as a 4th grader is who you'll be the rest of your life. If we're
to get to organizational leaders during the formative portions of
this level, we need to start at age 10, while moral plasticity is
present.

The Conventional level includes two stages, "Interpersonal
Concordance" (stage 3) and "Law and Order" (stage 4). A
significant difference between this and the preceding level is that

early childhood is significantly self-focused. But here we become far more aware of others and the importance of considering their views. In the third stage, right and wrong tend to be shaped by the majority as opposed to a narcissistic mindset. Stage four is about doing your duty for society, respecting authority, and complying with social laws. Although the goal would be to continue progressing through stage six, most end at four. The importance of beginning organizational skill training that includes character at age 10 is to do this at the transition from Level One to Level Two in moral development.

Following numerous corporate debacles in the 1970s, graduate business schools began adding ethics courses to their programs. While writing this book, our middle son, Josh, just finished an ethics course during his MBA at the University of Southern California. Certainly, teaching ethics at any age is valuable. But while these courses look good, for the most part they're window dressing. The reason is that by graduate school, our character is pretty much established. By college and high school, our moral fiber has gelled, even though our ability to articulate it verbally increases. It's not that we can't change, it's just that we rarely do, thus emphasizing the point that we need to get to organizational leaders while they're wet cement. As business people know, it's about ROI: return on investment.

Cognitive development. Jean Piaget is recognized for his early work in developmental psychology, primarily focusing on cognitions. His theory of development describes four stages. Concrete Operational is the third stage, spanning from ages 7 to 11 and characterized by problem-solving skills and inductive reasoning. During this time, a child's thought process becomes more adult-like in terms of using logic and lower levels of critical thinking. Inductive reasoning involves making inferences from observations that help them create generalizations. That's why this is referred to as concrete, in that they understand when they see it and experience it. That's why project-based training makes sense here because they learn best by doing. Merely talking about leadership and its many components is far too conceptual at this point. Another cognitive change is reduced egocentrism, so that children become more conversant and begin learning how to gain others' perspectives and ideas. These are vital to organizational behaviors.

Stage four is called Formal Operational, transcending from ages 12 through adulthood. This includes the transition from concrete to conceptual thinking. Students are able to solve problems through trial and error and strategizing, much more like scientists. They begin thinking deductively, developing hypotheses and alternatives in problem solving. Because of what is happening in their self-perception, they're more apt to consider their role with others and begin thinking more deeply about their purpose and uniqueness. So another reason for focusing on O Factors during the 10/13 Window is to prepare them as organizational leaders in the transition from concrete to conceptual thinking, since so much of leading others is conceptual in nature but with concrete results.

Dr. Jay Giedd, a neuroscientist at the National Institute of Mental Health, describes brain development around this time as blossoming and pruning:

> In the frontal part of the brain, the part of the brain involved in judgment, organization, planning, strategizing -- those very skills that teens get better and better at -- this process of thickening of the gray matter peaks at about age 11 in girls and age 12 in boys, roughly about the same time as puberty. After that peak, the gray matter thins as the excess connections are eliminated or pruned. So much of our research is focusing on trying to understand what influences or guides the building-up stage when the gray matter is growing extra branches and connections and what guides the thinning or pruning phase when the excess connections are eliminated. I think the exuberant growth during the pre-puberty years gives the brain enormous potential. The capacity to be skilled in many different areas is building up during those times.[2]

Pyscho-social development: Erik Erikson is noted for his work in the area of psycho-social development. He believed that people go through eight "crises" in the process of understanding who they are as individuals and their role in society. The first five pertain to ages 0-18 and the other three to adulthood. Like Freud, he believed that these are epigenic, meaning they are sequential and build upon each other. Stage four in this model spans years 5-12 and the psychosocial crisis is Industry versus Inferiority. The basic virtue (residual quality) is Competency. At this level, children begin developing autonomy and self-discipline. Those who become competent with skills that are recognized as worthwhile to others develop a sense of confidence. Those who do not feel inferior.

During years 12-18, youth experience the fifth crisis, titled
Identity vs. Role Confusion. The basic virtue focused on in this
stage is Fidelity. During the process, youth begin finding their
place within society at large and discovering what role they'll fill as
adults. Those who understand what they are good at enhance their
sense of identity. Those who do not ("I don't know what I want to
do when I grow up") become confused about the role they'll fill in
society as adults. When a student is successful, the result is the
virtue of fidelity, referring to the ability to commit to others and
accept them in spite of differences.

Age (Yrs)	5	6	7	8	9	10	11	12	13	14 -18
Kohlberg[3]	Preconven-tional					Conventional				
Piaget[4]						Concrete Operational				Formal Operational
Erikson[5]					Industry vs. Inferiority (Competence)					Identity vs. Role Confusion (Fidelity)

Table 2.0 Fundamental Developmental Stages

In addition to these foundational theories on human
development, we factored in Dr. Robert Epstein's research of
adolescence through history.[6] He notes that what we call
adolescence is a relative modern construct, only emerging in
Western society after 1800. Prior to that and throughout history,
14-year-olds were considered adults in that they began their careers

and building their family. They worked directly with adults as opposed to investing large amounts of time with peers in concentrated environs, such as public education that did not yet exist. As a result of this shift, social-emotional development has ebbed as teens spent less time with older adults and more time with peers, creating an extension of childhood that masks physical and responsibility maturation. He goes on to say that the reason for so much rebellion during teenage years in recent history is because we infantilize our youth, treating them like infants when they are physically, sexually, and cognitively capable of functioning as adults and have throughout history. Consider that a majority of the rite-of-passage rituals (i.e. Confirmation, Bar Mitzvah and Bat Mitzvah, the Aboriginal walkabout) happen on or by year 14. But by keeping youth home to allow for greater education to exist in a complex world, we create a sense of extended childhood. When I talked to Dr. Epstein, he explained what youth today need and want most is not more freedom, but rather more responsibility, thus dignifying them with significant roles in society and honoring them for their ideas and abilities. Organizational leadership development is a means of providing this. So you can see, the 10/13 Window is a strategic developmental opportunity.

Most who teach elementary school recognize a significant jump in cognitive and socio-emotional maturity at age 10. Our work with O Factors globally over the last decade concurs with this. We've noticed that a 9-year-old leading a project-based, organizational skill activity does not respond nearly as well as a similarly gifted 10-year-old. We've also noticed that in general, there's a significant attitude change among 14-year-olds, whereby they begin behaving more like high schoolers than middle schoolers. Perhaps it is based on how youth are socialized, at least here in the United States. That is why we designed two of our curricula programs for ages 10-13 (LeadNow) and 14-18 (LeadWell).

I want to reiterate that leadership development at any age, so long as it's well designed, is a good thing. But if we want to develop effective AND ethical leaders, we need to get to them while they're pliable. The target is years 10-18, but the bullseye is the 10/13 Window.

Developmental Qualities of the 10/13 Window[7]

Cognitive/Intellectual

* Increased ability to learn and apply skills

* Learning to extend thinking beyond personal experiences and knowledge

* Start viewing world outside of black-white/right-wrong perspective

* Interpretive ability develops, recognizing cause and effect sequences

* Beginning of abstract thinking

Emotional/Social

* Increased ability to interact with peers

* Developing and testing values and beliefs that guide present and

---

future behaviors

* Increased ability to engage in competition

* Strong group identity; increasingly defines self through peers

* Acquiring sense of accomplishment based on achievement

* Defines self-concept in part by success in school and socially

Physical

* Developing body proportions similar to those of an adult

* May begin puberty—development of sexuality (voice changes, increased body odor)

In the next chapter, we'll look at a variety of ways that adults inadvertently diminish the development of organizational leadership skills in O Factors.

Endnotes:

1. Velsor, E. V. and Wright, J. "Expanding the leadership equation: developing next-generation leaders" white paper (2012). Center for Creative Leadership, Greensboro, NC.

2. "Inside the teenage brain," an interview with Dr. Jay Giedd. Public Broadcasting Service (PBS) http://www.pbs.org/wgbh/pages/frontline/shows/teenbrain/interviews/gie dd.html 2002.

3. Kohlberg, L. (1981). The philosophy of moral development: Moral stages and the idea of justice (Vol. 1). San Francisco: Harper & Row.

4. Piaget, J. (1969, 2000). The psychology of the child. New York: Basic Books.

5. Erikson, E. H. (1950). Childhood and society. New York: Norton Pub.

6. Epstein, R. (2010). Teen 2.0. Fresno, CA: Quill Driver Books.

7. National Resource Center for Family-Centered Practice and Permanency Planning, Hunter College School of Social Work, New York, NY.

Chapter 7

How do we unintentionally hinder O Factors?

We cannot always build the future for our youth, but we can build the youth for our future.

-Franklin D. Roosevelt

Good Intentions, Bad Outcomes

"Watch your step," my dad warned, as we walked down the rows of the newly planted cornfield. "You don't want to crush the new corn." Growing up on a farm, I learned how delicate corn sprouts were. In a few weeks, the stalks would be stout enough to endure windstorms and adult work boots, but sprouts can be easily trampled. The same is true with young leaders.

A friend of mine, who is a respected leader, told me this story.

The other day I was at a youth sporting event with my dad, watching one of my teenage sons preparing for his game. He was kind of goofing around, having fun as he warmed up, exuding confidence. As I sat beside my father, he asked, "Who's Bradley most like?"

"He's most like me, Dad," I responded.

Then my dad startled me when he said, "No he's not. You're quiet."

I didn't say anything, but I realized at that moment that although I'm a leader at work, whenever I get around my dad, I get very quiet, much the way I did as a child.

The reason is that my friend's dad was a domineering, Type-A person, who demanded compliance and obedience from his kids growing up. Although my friend was indeed a leader as a child, when he expressed his opinions and personal views as a leader-child, they were considered rebellious by his strict, overbearing father. Therefore, my friend became reserved and passive as a boy at home, even though at school and other settings he was outgoing and considered a leader. The father perceived that his son had a quiet, retiring personality, never realizing how he'd snuffed out his son's leadership potential at home. When I tell this story in my parent and teacher training, nearly every time there are people in the audience who nod their heads. They relate to it because they too experienced the retribution of a parent or significant adult who did not understand their leadership attributes as a child and tried to eradicate them. Whether it is insecurity, ignorance, or any number of other personal issues, many adults hamper the development of budding leaders, causing them to withdraw into emotional caves.

If you confronted the domineering father in the story above, no doubt you'd experience disbelief and remorse that he responded in such a way to stifle his son's leadership abilities. But every day, scores of young leaders around the world duck into emotional closets in order to survive a world dominated by people who do not understand how to develop a young person with strong leadership wiring. Like a young bird that gets pecked at for flapping its wings, these leaders become frustrated and confused by the way they're treated by elders.

The purpose of this chapter is to educate adults, not make them feel guilty. But when we shut down O Factors for expressing their gifts, we set them back. Many late bloomers are merely leaders who've crawled into their shells because significant people in their lives condemned them for what came natural to them. Only after years of maturing and experiencing situations where their leading is rewarded do they become comfortable in their own skin. The following are five of the most common ways that adults shut down the natural expression of youthful leaders as they begin to experiment with their strengths.

5 Ways to Break an O Factor's Spirit

1. Poor listening and exclusion of their ideas.
You could argue that poor listening skills and an exclusion of ideas would diminish the self-esteem and confidence of any child, but it's even more pronounced with O Factors. Here's why. As we mentioned prior, organizational leaders have a lot of opinions and ideas. That is one of their strengths. So when we shut them out of conversations, tell them to be quiet and consistently make decisions without allowing their input, we've pretty much communicated, "Your opinions aren't worth hearing. Your strength is not valued in this family, classroom, or team."

One way we train adults to discern possible peer leaders is to think about people who share opinions with them. Having an opinion does not make you a leader. You may merely be opinionated. But organizational leaders do have a lot of opinions. Their minds are constantly churning, responding internally to people, situations, and possibilities. When non-leaders who are in charge have people around them like this, they often ostracize them as troublemakers, labeling them as negative and critical, but savvy people recognize that these people might be frustrated leaders who want to be heard. They can capitalize on their influence by embracing instead of alienating them.

Ratchet that back a few years and you find children and youth who have a lot of views on various things. Adults fear letting these children air these views because they think that if a young leader expresses an opinion, s/he will take over. Just like adults, though, what O Factors value most is having their voices heard. By allowing people to express their ideas, we help them process their thinking and build consensus, and we also esteem them for thinking. We'll often find, if we're humble, that O Factors come up with some really great ideas that will improve whatever it is we're doing. For example, when we were selecting logos for KidLead, we let a group of preteens in one of our LeadNow programs select the logo we now use.

Generally, girls are more verbal than boys. You can see the difference very early. They tend to process life by verbalizing thoughts and ideas. Again, when we expect our daughters to be seen and not heard, dismissing their ideas and merely hearing but not listening to them, we devalue what they bring to society as leaders. Responding to the ideas of young O Factors requires emotional intelligence. While we can't always provide ample time and attention for listening, when we consistently quiet our kids, exclude them from adult conversations, and dismiss their ideas as childish because they're young, we telegraph the idea that their natural gifting is not valued. By failing to reinforce their opinions, we communicate that their leadership is not valid. Literally, we're creating leader "invalids."

2. Treating siblings and peers the same.

Talk to almost any parent with multiple children, and you'll hear them say, "They're so different from each other." Kevin Lehman is an expert in the field of birth order. He's the bestselling author of *The Birth Order Book* and a good book on children leaders titled *The First Born Advantage*. In his years of research, Lehman has determined that in addition to personalities and gender, birth order can influence a child's wiring. Obviously, gender and personality play into the differences. Anyone who's raised both girls and boys recognizes how unique each is. Despite parents' acknowledgement that their children are different, they often try to treat them the same to be fair. If we fail to distinguish differences and respond to them appropriately, we do a disservice to our children, even though our intent is to treat them fairly.

That is what the Marland Report points out that a problem of an egalitarian culture is that we mistake equal value with equal ability. When we confuse these, we overlook those with unique gifts and talents who need to be developed differently for them to reach their potential. When schools treat everyone the same, they do a disserve to those who are not the same. So while we mean well, this strategy is inherently flawed.

This is true in general and especially when it comes to raising kids with organizational leadership aptitude. Although we'll deal with this more in the next few chapters, the point here is that if you try to treat all of your children the same, you'll fail to develop them according to their potential. It's similar to an employer reacting to all of his employees alike or a saleswoman relating to her customers the same way. The most effective supervisors and service people respond to people as individually as possible. While you retain the same values for all family members, you'll want to create unique and effective learning opportunities. This is but another thing that makes good parenting difficult, because you need to be adaptable based on what will benefit each child the most.

For example, in order to help a compliant child learn self-discipline, the ultimate goal of discipline, sometimes all you need to do is give a stern look. This modest feedback immediately changes the behavior of the compliant personality. But if you're trying to raise a leader who is strong-willed, she will not benefit from such a passive approach. This child needs more assertive, intentional, in-your-face discipline— that still allows feedback—to register at the same level on his or her response meter.

For example, children who are nervous typically need more nurturing and empathy then their risk-taking siblings, who may benefit more from warnings and guidelines. The goal is to create confidence in both children, but the methods for accomplishing this differ. Leader-types benefit from gaining confidence through opportunities that allow them to test drive their leadership by overseeing projects and experimenting with new ideas. One thing we learned from effective leader parents we interviewed for this book is that they try to have consistent, one-on-one time with their children. This allows the parent to tailor fit interactions based on the uniqueness of each child.

3. Intimidating with threats and verbal warnings.
   ("I'm the boss around here." "I'm the teacher in this class.")
   If you've ever walked down the aisle at Wal-Mart or your local grocery store, you've probably heard a parent aggressively scolding a child who is misbehaving. You'll hear threats of punishment and irate responses from a parent who feels out of control. If you've

ever seen the television show Super Nanny, you've seen examples of parents' lives being managed by budding leaders running amuck. We've all been there as parents, hanging on to the end of our rope after a long day at work or herding kids. But when this parenting style becomes your default mode, chances are, you're diminishing the leadership abilities of your children. This is most common among two types of parents and teachers: those who are not leaders themselves but have leader-type kids/students, and those who are leaders but who lack sufficient emotional intelligence to handle an immature leader trying to stretch his or her wings. The result is butting heads, battling for control. The adults feel overwhelmed. In order to diminish the young leader's power, they try to intimidate with verbal or physical force. The goal is tension reduction.

Helping O Factors gain confidence and self-discipline is a difficult process. It requires very intentional concentration on saying and doing the right things at strategic times called teachable moments. These are situations of failure, conflict, and discipline, where you are able to attach consequences to actions and attitudes. Don't rush the process if possible. Push "pause" and discuss the various parts or perceptions leading up to the situation. When you play the "parent or teacher card" in order to gain control and get your way, it usually means you've lost the battle. This is a last resort strategy. When this becomes your standard mode of parenting, classroom supervision or team coaching, your O Factor has lost the opportunity to develop his or her organizational leadership potential while in your midst. Leaders, more than others, want to feel respected for what they bring to the table and acknowledged for their ideas. They need a safe place to express their gifts of influence, where they can grow in confidence and fail with dignity.

4. Punishing vs. disciplining a creative and strong-willed O Factor.

While all mothers are women, not all women are mothers. The same logic goes for leaders. While most leaders possess strong wills, not all strong- willed students are leaders. Therefore, handling a strong-willed O Factor may appear to be simply a parenting issue, but it is more than that. In the beginning of this chapter, we told the story of a middle-aged man who grew up with a dominant father whose overbearing parenting style stunted the young leader's development. While this leader was at home, he was very quiet and passive, but outside of the home, he was outgoing, clownish, and a student leader at school. Punishment discourages a child from expressing his or her basic personality. Discipline hones it so that it is appropriate. Punishment strives to extinguish a behavior with pain, physical or emotional. But for the most part, punishment is fear-oriented and temporary, primarily effective only when the threat of pain is present.

When you intimidate with verbal threats or punish students exhibiting outgoing creativity, you damage their leadership development. When this happens under age fourteen, you'll usually find a child who becomes passive in that environment, whether at home or school, wearing an emotional mask to survive around the authority figure. When this happens with O Factors over fourteen, you'll usually have adult-child contention and ultimately rebellion. The young organizational leader can't wait to exit the house or school and often does so as soon as possible with minimal looking back. Schools with disciplinary problems almost always fail to tap and develop the potential in their O Factors, labeling them as trouble makers and creating unnecessary power struggles that work against them.

Discipline, as opposed to punishment, has to do with self-awareness, self-control, and learning the reality of consequences. A primary reason why pastors have affairs, politicians take bribes, and business leaders cut illegal deals is because these leaders failed to learn self-discipline. These individuals failed to develop self-discipline early on in life, before their characters solidified. That is why it is so important to teach kids ethical behavior. After our moral compass is set, we're far less apt to adopt values and principles that differ from those we learned in childhood or as preteens. Delay of gratification is important for everyone, but it's crucial for leaders, whose decisions impact many other people and the organizations they serve.

Punishing rule breakers is a common dilemma in schools and families where compliance is highly valued, but one that curtails future organizational risk taking. Controlled environs can actually bring out the rebel in many an O Factor who is genetically predisposed to push the boundaries, because that's what leaders tend to do. Recent research has identified what they call a "naughty" gene, referring to the dopamine transporter gene, DAT1. This gene is noticeably present among many who occupy leadership positions.[1] These are the rule breakers, people who push the limits, don't comply with status quo, and resist accepting things as they are. The problem is that this same gene is also present among law breakers, those who go too far in resisting authority and don't seem to know when to comply. Studies show that adolescence who are rule breakers tend to rise in organizational leadership roles. The key is to not go too far.

5. Lack of intentional mentoring and training.

When a photographer sees a pastoral setting at sunset, she wants to capture it with her camera. When a coach sees an athlete with natural gifting, he wants him on the team so he can tap the talent. When a teacher finds a student with incredible promise, she creates opportunities to challenge the pupil. People look for opportunities like these all the time. But what do we do when we see a young child with natural leadership gifts? Most of the time, we do nothing. At best, we say, "Someday, you're going to be a leader." Ignoring a child's unique gift of influence can retard his or her progress if we miss key developmental periods. That is why we've invested so much time and energy into LeadYoung Training Systems, a program that we've designed for ten- to twenty-five-year-olds. When adults fail to recognize and esteem this unique ability, we convey the idea that it is not important, diminishing the O Factor's sense of value.

Why Adults Fail to Develop O Factors

Parents and adults overlook intentional mentoring and training due to a few common reasons. One is that they don't recognize leadership gifting indicators. As we've mentioned, parents confuse leadership aptitude with being rebellious, strong-willed, bossy, opinionated, overly confident, or outgoing. Some misperceive academic excellence with leading. Misdiagnosis is dangerous in medicine as well as child development. While we have programs such as youth athletics, arts, and academics that reveal aptitude in these areas, we rarely find venues for assessing leadership aptitude. Leaders, therefore, often don't see these abilities in themselves as students until they look back as adults.

Another is that adults assume leadership development will emerge later on its own. Because our culture believes that leading is an adult activity, we perceive it is not our responsibility to develop latent talent. Instead, we assume that we've done our work by merely raising our kids responsibly and getting them to college or their first job. Then it's life or corporations that will train them how to lead. Thus, we procrastinate leadership development among children and youth.

What the gifted and talented movement has discovered is that these students need intentional development to flourish. Traditionally, very little funding goes toward GT programs because we assume that since they're gifted, they'll figure it out by themselves. (In the US, reports show that about 2 cents of every $100 spent on education goes toward programs for those with exceptional abilities.) Rather, we pour our money into those struggling. While it's fine to make sure not child gets "left behind," it's a shame that we don't help our most talented get ahead. The Marland Report and subsequent studies reveal that neglecting the upper end of the talent spectrum does thwart their progress. That is why some educational systems include gifted and talented in their "Special Ed" programs because they recognize something unique is required to help them reach their potential.

Yet another reason adults fail to develop O Factors is that they don't have the skills needed to differentiate organizational leadership development from normal parenting and teaching. That is the primary reason for this book. We want to help parents, teachers, and coaches craft their abilities in detecting, developing, and deploying young organizational leaders. Most of us never saw executive skills modeled when we were young, let alone received any formal training regarding youth leadership development.

One more reason adults overlook developing O Factors is that they lack adequate tools, programs, and resources designed to hone both character and competencies. Nearly all of the programs calling themselves leadership are really more about parenting, community service, self-esteem, and character. Up to now, all serious leadership programs and resources have focused on adults. Those with a youth emphasis tend to be generic programs that fail to distinguish those children with natural aptitude, yet they label them leadership because it sells.

When a parent sees that his child has exceptional soccer ability, he will try to find a club or competitive team where the level of play and coaching will likely develop the child's potential. Chances are it will cost more time and money, but recreational soccer leagues will not help the child improve significantly. The same is true whether it is sports, arts, science, or any number of other unique gifts and abilities. This is the reason for AP classes and gifted and talented programs in schools, to provide special development opportunities for academic success. Leadership should be no different.

Good News

History is full of stories of young leaders who were overlooked, misunderstood, and had any inclination of leadership beaten out of them, sometimes literally. Many children gifted as leaders are wrongly diagnosed and defeated by well-intentioned adults who either do not understand their unique wiring or fail to know what to do with it when it is exhibited.

Far too many resources flow toward fixing social problems. They are reactionary in nature, consuming billions of dollars and hundreds of thousands of hours. Leadership development, especially among young leaders, is primarily preventative. If we identified and proactively trained young leaders, we'd reduce the number of gang leaders, curtail future CEO scandals, and decrease organizational floundering that results when leaders go bad. Besides that, more and better leaders would address the remaining problems with greater confidence and diligence. We invest far too much effort on squeaky wheels in society, wondering why we seem to make little headway over the long haul.

In the next chapter, we'll look at a unique 4-year window in the developmental process when we're most apt to succeed in building effective and ethical organizational leadership skills.

Endnotes:

1. Li, W. D., Wang, N., Arvey, R. D., Soong, R., Saw, S. M., &
   Song, Z. (2015). A mixed blessing? Dual mediating
   mechanisms in the relationship between dopamine transporter
   gene DAT1 and leadership role occupancy. *The Leadership
   Quarterly.*

Chapter 8

How can we develop O Factors?

Tell me, I forget.
Teach me, I might remember.
Involve me, I understand.

There are three common situations where O Factors fail to be developed. One is where a non-leader-parent, -teacher, or -coach fails to recognize leadership aptitude in a child or misdiagnoses it as a rebellious attitude. A second is where a leader-parent, -teacher, or -coach overwhelms the young leader, is unwilling to share power, and intimidates the budding leader into compliance. The third scenario is where both non-leader and leader recognize leadership ability in a child but don't know how to develop it. They hope that someone, someday, somehow will recognize and unleash the latent potential in the young influencer.

The good news is that whether you're a leader or not, you can grow the O Factors around you. That is the big idea of this book. In this chapter, you'll discover 8 Great Practices to begin doing this. While these are best suited for parents or guardians, others who work with O Factors can adapt them. We'll dedicate a specific chapter for developmental activities in the home (Chapter 10) and offer educators more ideas for creating leader-friendly classrooms in Chapter 12.

8 Great Practices

1. *Imagine your O Factor as an adult leader.*

We've said before, but every great adult leader throughout history was at one time a 10 and 14 year old. Look beyond the current age and see his or her potential. Leadership development of your child begins between your ears, how you think about him or her. As a parent, you will be the most influential person in the life of your child, at least until college and often beyond. Therefore, while you want to enjoy your children at every stage of their development, imagine them grown up. See your child as a person who someday will be hired, will hire and influence others. All too often, we love our children but limit them by the way we see them. We continue to picture them as the helpless babes they were when we first met them, thus overlooking their unique strengths and aptitudes.

One of the benefits we've seen in **LeadNow** preteen training modules is that the Certified Trainers and *Koaches* (our term for adult team coaches) often do not know the *Leaders* (our term for ten- to thirteen- year-old participants) very well. That means we don't see them as kids. We visualize them as future CEOs, presidents, community activists, and entrepreneurs. Because our culture considers leading primarily as an adult behavior, most parents rarely see the ability of their children to lead as young people. If a child seems to have organizational leadership ability, then the next step is not about them, it's how YOU think about them.

2. Treat your O Factor as a young leader; inexperienced but fully capable.

The reason why we need to begin seeing our children as organizational leaders is because this will directly affect how we treat them. How we treat them influences how they see themselves and as a result, how they react. This is known as the Pygmalion effect, which says that people become as they are treated. The term refers to a story from Greek mythology, based on the name of a sculptor who crafted an ivory statue of a beautiful woman. He treated the sculpture as if it were alive, giving it gifts, dressing it with a necklace and caressing it. After saying a prayer to the goddess Aphrodite, she turned the sculpture into a live woman, whom Pygmalion then married.

When we begin treating our O Factors as the organizational leaders they can become, we'll see them respond as leaders. "Alexa, you're a leader. How would a good leader respond in this situation?" "Jason, I want you to be a leader when your friends come over, so what can you do to organize some activities?" Obviously, merely calling your child a leader is insufficient, but as you begin providing opportunities that support your words, you will see behavior change. This is one of the most amazing transformations we see after just a few training sessions in *LeadNow*, where the preteen O Factors are expected to lead their peers in activities that begin to change their self-images and thus their speech and behavior.

3. Discuss leadership situations as they arise from school, news, movies, and work.

Nearly every day, you'll have life events, stories, and media that provide opportunities to talk about leadership, whether in brief sound bites or more prolonged discussions. The goal is to make your child aware of situations where leaders influence others – for good and for bad—in order to create an unconscious orientation so that they can "read" leadership situations. For example, let's say that your child comes home from school and tells you about a food fight that broke out in the cafeteria.

"It was amazing," Cyndi says. "Bobby Nanson and Jonny Carol started throwing French fries at each other. Then a whole bunch of people started tossing things from their lunches. Then the principal walked in and got really mad. He made a lot of people stay after school and clean up the lunch room."

As a parent, you could say something such as, "My goodness. You didn't throw any food, did you?" Or you might react, "That's terrible. It's a good thing they got in trouble."

But if you changed hats from parent to leadership coach, you might respond, "So why do you think the other kids started throwing food? Do you think they did it just because Bobby and Jonny did? Do kids follow Bobby and Jonny in other situations, like in class or the playground?" If the answer is "yes," then ask, "Why do you think they follow them?" "Do you think their decision to start throwing food was a good one or not?" "Why do you think that?"

The goal is neutral, matter-of-fact conversation, helping your child begin thinking about social influencers and raising his or her awareness of leadership situations.

In another scenario, you're driving home from the movie *Shrek 2* with your child and a few friends. You might ask, "What do you think about the scene when the King met Shrek? How did the King treat Shrek? How do you think the King's response made Shrek feel? Why is a leader's response to people so important?"

Notice that you're not lecturing, condemning, criticizing, or giving answers. You're asking strategic questions. In our LeadYoung Trainer Certification, we teach trainers not to talk more than 25% of the time during Team Time discussions. This is the period after an activity when the team debriefs to discuss the concept being learned as well as how the team functioned. One thing we've discovered, especially among ten- and eleven-year-olds, is that they expect the adult to have the answer and do most of the talking. But after a few club meetings, when the preteens are asked questions and given unrushed time to talk, they gain confidence and begin sharing their ideas.

Here's one more scenario. You're with your daughter but talking on your phone with a colleague about a situation at work that your boss seems to be handling poorly. You don't like it that a few individuals seem to be getting away with working less, requiring you and your partners to cover their responsibilities, while your supervisor turns his head. After you hang up from the call, you say nothing or you mutter with disgust, "That's so unfair. Our boss isn't doing his job."

You could also turn to your daughter, briefly explain the situation, and then ask questions, such as: "What do you think about that?" "What do you think we should do?" "Have you ever had a teacher or coach

who didn't seem to be treating everyone the same?"
"Why do you think leaders do that?" And if you're really
confident, you can ask, "Can you think of a time when I
treated you that way or gave preferred treatment to your
brother or sister? If so, when was it and how could I
improve?"

What you're doing is communicating the idea that
leaders aren't perfect but can learn. Leaders must become aware
of others' feeling and treat people on their teams fairly, or at
least explain why someone may or may not be carrying as much
of the workload. You are also teaching your child, whether you
realize it or not, how to lead up, influencing those with greater
authority and power. If you act like a victim, then you're
training your child to be a complainer. If you are taking a
proactive, assertive approach to addressing the situation,
you're showing her how she can influence positively even if she's
not the boss.

Every day, situations arise in your family members' lives
and in the media that create teachable moments when you can
initiate mini- discussions about leaders and how people
influence each other. You may not always get a lot of response
from your children, but don't underestimate the benefit of them
thinking about what you say and learning how to analyze a
leadership situation.

4. *Develop organizational leadership projects at home.*

This is a powerful strategy to make organizational leadership
skill development a significant part of your weekly schedule,
without necessarily going out of your way to create situations
separate from your ongoing lifestyle. We've committed an entire
chapter to these ideas (Chapter 10), but wanted to list it as one of

the eight great practices.

5. *Find opportunities for organizational leading in the community.*

Creating organizational leadership projects in the home can naturally evolve into similar situations in the community. This is where a budding organizational leader can gain significant confidence. As you begin getting into the neighborhood and organizations with which you're familiar, you also help other adults grasp the idea that child and youth leaders can make a significant difference on their own.

Begin with organizations where you and/or your student have familiarity. This might be a faith community, school, athletic team, or immediate neighborhood. Talk with the adult in charge and ask about needs or small projects that could use a hand. Most nonprofits have a variety of small tasks that get overlooked at any given time. Your questions may catch the people in charge off guard, so you may need to brainstorm ideas with them or perhaps ask them to think about it. Obviously, you need to keep in mind the age of the O Factor, the difficulty of the project, and what it might take to accomplish the tasks. You'll want to begin small as your young leader gains confidence.

The key, as in all organizational leadership projects, is that you have a clear objective, that there are multiple people involved, and that you truly let the O Factor lead, as opposed to telling him or her what to do and then merely calling the task leadership.

In organizations using our LeadYoung training curriculum, students have led others in collecting school supplies for needy kids, raising money for child advocacy homes, organizing recycling

111

drives in schools, and convincing a principal to change school policy due to a bully causing havoc on the playground. We offer more ideas on projects like these at the KidLead website (www.kidlead.com). Unless you have someone from the organization supervising the project, you may need to be available to serve as a coach, who may or may not choose to be on the team. You'll be tempted to take over at times and tell the O Factors what to do, but try to avoid this unless a decision related to safety issues. We'll talk more about coaching skills in the next chapter.

A growing number of schools require community service from their students. This is a wonderful trend that helps students experience giving back, without pay, to those in need. The big difference between most community service opportunities and organizational leadership training is that the former are done as individuals or followers. But when an O Factor organizes and supervises peers and even adults, they learn about leading.

Again, make sure that you provide feedback times at the end when youth can think about what went well, what didn't go well, and what they might improve next time. Articulating what did and didn't go well, how people worked together, and other aspects of the project, takes learning to a much higher level.

6. *Introduce your O Factor to other leaders.*

Leaders recognize other leaders. O Factors will have a certain amount of natural affinity with other organizational leaders, regardless of their age. When you are meeting someone who is a leader in his or her organization or field, go out of your way to have your student meet this person. While many parents still exhibit the "children should be seen, not heard" attitude, at least when it comes to meeting people of power and

112

organizational importance, this anxiety is based more on their own insecurity. I've found that most leaders do well meeting children, especially kids with leadership aptitude, because adult leaders see it in them as well. Adult leaders feel honored, and the really good ones focus on the child, looking her eye to eye and shaking her hand. You know you've met a good leader when s/he gets down to your child's eye level and begins conversing with the young leader, ignoring you for the moment.

In one situation reported in the Bible, Jesus scolded his handlers for keeping the children away from him. He said, "Hey, let the kids come to me. I want to meet them. You can learn a lot from them." When our oldest son, Jeff, was a junior in college, he was thinking about becoming a psychologist. At the time, I was interviewing a bestselling author who was a psychologist, for a magazine I worked for as executive editor. I called Jeff and said, "I'm meeting with Dr. Cloud. Would like you to drop by for five minutes and meet him?"

I purchased one of Dr. Cloud's books and introduced him to Jeff. He autographed the book for Jeff, and I took their picture as they talked briefly. The whole episode took less than five minutes, but it was a way of esteeming Jeff as well as introducing him to a leader in his field of interest. We've done this dozens of times over the years as opportunities have arisen. While it often requires pre-thinking and a little extra organization, the results are worth it.

Obviously, you need to be sensitive to both your child and the leader you want him to meet. It may be appropriate to ask the leader's permission or say, "I'd love to have my son meet you briefly, if that's okay." Again, this type of invitation is seen more as an honor than a burden for most leaders. Savvy leaders are good at the politics of relationships; they understand that family ties and friendships are important parts of getting things done, and they know the importance of conveying that they are approachable, friendly, and humble. Good leaders accomplish this with authenticity.

7. Help your O Factor find a mentor.

All of us as parents are limited in what we can provide for our children when it comes to modeling and communicating experiences. The statement is well-worn but true, "It takes a village to raise a child." One thing parents can do to nurture their young leader is help them find mentors who lead in different types of organizations and with varying styles. We'll discuss this more in the next chapter, but it deserves to be in the 8 Great Practices list.

8. *Seek formal and informal leadership training.*

When we detect musical talent, we get our child music lessons. When we discern academic ability, we move them toward AP classes and gifted and talented programs. When we observe athletic ability, we hire coaching from a pro and seek competitive-level teams. The challenge most parents face when they see leadership aptitude in their students is finding any semblance of concentrated leadership training. Very little exists that teaches organizational leader character and executive skills. That's why we designed LeadYoung Training Systems curricula. We'll share more about this formal training in the last chapter, but you'll find a plethora of informal ideas in subsequent chapters that offer a template for developing your own at home, in school and the community.

So whether you're a parent, guardian, educator, coach or youth worker, there are plenty of opportunities to develop the O Factors around you. These 8 Great Practices involve some of the more general ones, but we'll expand on these in subsequent chapter for parents and educators. The bottom line is that it should be intentional, not haphazard.

In the next chapter, we'll look specifically at the skill of coaching, to show how O Factors need to be groomed differently than the way most adults instruct students, by telling them what to do or think.

Chapter 9

How do we coach O Factors?

People make history and not the other way around. In periods where there are no leaders, society stands still. Progress occurs when courageous, skillful leaders seize the opportunity to change things for the better.

-Harry S. Truman

Perhaps the biggest mistake adults make with O Factors, after failing to recognize they can lead, is bumping against the young leader's will. That is why understanding the differences between parenting/teaching and coaching an O Factors is invaluable. If you apply some basic skills and adopt the attitude of an executive coach, you'll save yourself a lot of headaches and frustration. If anything, consider this chapter a survival guide on handling budding organizational leaders. This chapter is written in the context of parenting, but feel free to substitute the role you play in the life of an O Factor, should you be a teacher, youth worker, coach or other family member.

Know Your and Your O Factor's Leadership Styles

You don't have to be a leadership expert to recognize that there are a variety of leadership styles. While many popular personality assessments focus on four predominant temperaments, these also emerge in terms of leading styles. They are Director, Inspirer, Strategist and Collaborator. Understanding these basic styles helps adults assess themselves as well as young leaders. There is no right or wrong style. All can be effective when used properly. These are natural tendencies and typically do not change over time although leaders can vary them temporarily, depending on the situation.

Adult leaders often mistakenly assume that their leadership style is the only correct way to lead, and they try to shape young leaders to fit that mold. All four dominant styles have unique strengths and weaknesses. When we force a style unnatural to a young leader, we make her susceptible to displaying the weaknesses instead of the strengths, since the strengths are more difficult to adopt.

I write and eat left-handed. Fortunately my parents did not try to switch me to the right hand, but I've heard several frustrated left- handers whose teachers or parents did. Like preferred hand use, leaders have a preferred style that feels right to them. It is wise to help a young leader develop in that style and not necessarily adopt a different preferred style of someone else. This requires learning the differences among the four leadership styles and not pushing ours onto our children. To accomplish this we need to implement emotional intelligence and coaching skills as we help a young leader with a different leading style develop his or her own. The following is a summary of four common leadership styles.

Director: This style is the stereotypical leader who emerges quickly, exuding direction and confidence.

Strengths:

•Decisive: quickly chooses a preferred course

•Visionary: imagines a preferred outcome

•Bold: willing to take risks

Weaknesses:

*Bossy: can alienate others

*Isolation: may make decisions alone

*Naïve: may overlook team input

Inspirer: This style motivates followers to feel good about participating in a cause greater than themselves.

Strengths:

•Motivational: is engaging and inspiring

•Encouraging: makes people feel good about themselves

•Positive: creates hope by seeing possibilities

Weaknesses:

*Fickle: may not follow through

*Impulsive: may not consider costs

*Talker: may seek too much attention

Strategist: This style is calculating and thoughtful, more reserved in communication but well suited for problem solving.

Strengths:

•Organized: thinks in systems

•Thorough: thinks through details

•Sensitive: alert to the feelings of others

Weaknesses:

*Negative: may be fearful of failure

*Perfectionist: can procrastinate or focus on negative

*Mired: can get stuck figuring out every detail

Collaborator: This style gets along well with people and is good at reconciliation, negotiating, and team building.

Strengths:

• Relational: likes and is liked by people

• Stable: is steady and even-keeled emotionally

• Peaceful: is good at conveying balance

Weaknesses:

*Procrastinates: can be lazy

*Reticent: can resist taking risks

*Inoffensive: may avoid confrontation

As you look at the brief lists of strengths and weaknesses, what would you say is your preferred organizational leadership style, and what is the natural style of your young O Factor? You may want to ask a few people who know you well for different perspectives. How is your style the same or different from your student's, and what might be some possible differences that could either cause conflict or tempt you to try and change your child's style to be more like your own? For example, I am more of a Director but my oldest son, Jeff, is more of a Collaborator. From time to time, I've been tempted to get Jeff to be more like me, to lead as a decisive visionary. But one of Jeff's strengths is his ability to get along with people, avoid unnecessary conflict, and succeed by creating social ties.

Comparing Aptitude Strengths

In addition to identifying and contrasting leadership styles, it is also helpful for parents to estimate and contrast leadership aptitude strengths. The reason is that when there is a mismatch in terms of natural capacity between you and your O Factor, there will naturally be tension issues unless you consciously adapt.

In the beginning of this book, we discussed leadership aptitude, a young person's natural capacity to learn how to lead. During our LeadYoung trainer certification, we show trainers how to estimate aptitude on a one to five scale. Applicants with a one or two value are encouraged to wait for further development, lest they not benefit sufficiently from the training. Those determined to be a three are said to be "on the bubble," meaning they may or may not be invited to participate, pending the number of Trainers and Koaches in the club and the level of other applicants' aptitudes. Those most likely to be invited into the training are fours and fives because they can make the most of the training.

While it may sound logical to suggest that those with lower numbers could benefit more, this is not the case, because capacity to learn tends to coincide with our natural strengths. Every person only has a few strengths. As we've mentioned, the responsibility of adults is to help children and youth discover and develop these individual aptitudes. Leader strength varies among adults as well, but by adulthood, we've usually had sufficient opportunities to lead, so our capacity is better revealed. Generally, we exude a certain level of leadership. Think of it in terms of a thermos that holds influence. Some people are smaller in the amount of their influence, others are medium, and some are able to hold a lot. On a one to five scale, one being low and five being high, what would you say is your leadership strength?

Determining the degree of your strength and the aptitude of a child is important because the difference impacts how you coach an O Factor. An adult with a higher degree of leadership strength can easily intimidate a child, creating fear. The adult may discourage the young organizational leader and make the youth feel that s/he is not good enough. Strong leaders can bowl over and push people without knowing it. Their very presence can be imposing even if they throttle back their verbal commands and directions.

Just as a parent who was an outstanding college athlete may not understand why his child isn't hitting homeruns in little league, a strong leader can have too high of expectations for a young leader and stunt his growth. If your overall leadership strength is higher, you'll need to consciously throttle back your energy so that you don't overpower the young leader.

Conversely, if you have lower leader strength than your child's capacity, the weakness will be in not challenging her sufficiently. You'll be reticent when your preteen or teen needs more push. You may not think of situations where your child can gain leading experience because you're not inclined to come up with these intuitively. You'll need to intentionally throttle up the way you coach, speak of leadership, and encourage your child to lead. When it comes to the test of wills, stand strong. Don't let your budding leader overwhelm you, lest you lose her respect. Strong leaders need pushback at times. While it feels awkward at the moment, they admire you more than if you give into them.

All our sons play or played competitive tennis. When they were starting, I coached them, and I was better than they were. But there came a point when they began beating me. While I could keep hitting with them and taking them through drills, they'd surpassed my ability to coach them sufficiently. That's when we had to take them to teaching pros and line up superior players for practice.

Unless you are a skilled leader-coach or a strong leader yourself, it will be difficult to develop a young leader whose capacity to lead is greater than your own. Your support at some point will come by getting them connected with more dynamic training, mentoring, and experiences so they can develop more fully. Your emotional support is always vital, but it's important that you estimate your own limits as well as your child's.

The Fine Art of Disciplining an O Factor (ages 5-12)

An important goal of developing a young organizational leader is to help him or her become self-disciplined. This objective equips young leaders to handle power effectively. This is important for all children but vital in the life of a leader. When inner strength is missing, leaders succumb to power when sufficiently tempted. The consequences hurt them and the people they serve. Here are some ideas that are parent-oriented but pertain specifically to raising leaders.

1. Keep the rules simple.

Scores of miniscule regulations about eating, talking, cleaning, toys, television, and relationships are confusing. They can also turn kids into legalists who, when faced with situations without laws, will lack the ability to make ethical decisions. Leaders who learn rules over values are apt to finding loopholes and ways around rules that may get them and their organizations into trouble as adults. Teach values and then help them identify situations where these come into play. For example, in our family, we've primarily stressed three rules.

* We don't hurt people.

* We don't hurt things.

* We don't hurt ourselves.

2. Don't threaten with unrealistic consequences.

"If you don't come here right now, Mom's going to leave you." When you declare consequences that are not likely to happen, you teach an underlying belief that the child is above the law and can get away with things. This will be problematic as s/he ages and conveys that attitude toward company policy and legal authorities. Obviously, there are times when a responsible parent will mandate immediate behavior, but this should be a last resort versus the default. Select outcomes that are realistic to implement and then do so. Where possible, let natural consequences run their course. We mentioned this in Chapter 3 and noted how punishment tends to disempower leaders, while healthy discipline empowers them.

3. Provide options.

When you only give an O Factor one choice, yours, you unnecessarily frustrate an innate drive leaders have to make decisions. Most leaders possess a noncompliance gene. When you say something can't be done, they intuitively feel motivated to prove it can. For example, instead of saying, "Quit playing your video game and go to bed," you might say, "You have two options. It's nine o' clock. Either you can go to bed now and play your video game after school tomorrow, or you can stay up until ten and not play your video game the rest of the week. It's your choice." You haven't abdicated parenting because you've established parameters for the two options, but you provided a choice for your child. She will need to weigh the pros and cons, the outcomes, and then she will feel empowered to make the decision even if she may not enjoy the consequences either way. This is a challenge of leading. But your young leader feels esteemed by being offered a choice.

4. Use a graduated process for gaining desired behavior.

O Factors frequently possess strong wills. In the appropriate place, this is a valuable strength. But adults who jump to the conclusion that a child is being intentionally disrespectful and rebellious will create unnecessary conflict. Consider a graduated approach that doesn't assume the worst.

A. Get the child's attention by speaking his name. Wait for a response, and then ask for the desired behavior. This ensures communication has really happened.

B. Make eye contact and repeat your request. Ask the child to repeat what you said, and then acknowledge that you value "first time obedience" or "first time cooperation."

C. If behavior is still unacceptable, ask, "Can you get yourself under control, or do you need my help?" This communicates seriousness but in an honoring manner that leaves them in control

D. If this is ineffective, assume the child needs your assistance. Physically move him to comply, whether it is escorting her to a certain part of the room or helping her hold a ball that you asked her to stop bouncing.

E. As a last resort, remove her from the immediate environment and use this as a one-on-one opportunity to find out what's going on inside of her or talk "leadership" with her. Help her consider how her actions are impacting others and failing to reach the goal effectively.

This approach is generally effective from early childhood through preteens. After that, you need to respond as a boss or a superior because most teens possess the psyche of an adult even though they may not exhibit adult traits yet.

5.   Use signals, not public embarrassment, to ask for attention or control.

If you have an O Factor who consistently struggles with self-control, you may want to prearrange a communication system with her. Sometimes, adults try to embarrass young leaders in an attempt to belittle them publicly. This is the action of an adult who feels threatened and at a loss for more effective means. The problem is that while you may curtail their behavior temporarily, you're apt to damage the child's self-esteem and turn the influencer against you, causing further problems down the road.

Because organizational leaders are good at influencing peers, they are prone to be sensitive to how they are treated in front of others. By nature, they are pied pipers. When you encounter an influencer with little self-discipline, it is helpful to pre-establish a "secret" code that communicates your need for the immature leader to exhibit more self-control, without public humiliation. This sign could be tugging at your ear lobe as you look at the child, a light tap on the shoulder as you walk past her, or some other cue that is discreet.

Scott Blanchard, son of leadership gurus Ken and Margie Blanchard, on how his dad disciplined him.

Like many boys, I was not that interested in hearing other people's warnings or advice. I had the tendency of getting into mischief that grew over the years. One of the things that used to happen in my family, being raised by a leadership professor who was not yet guru status, along with my mom, who is a PhD, was how I was disciplined. I used to yearn to be punished like the kids down the street when they got into trouble, where they got restrictions, or grounded, or additional chores. My punishment involved sitting at the table and talking with my parents about how my behavior was incongruent with the stated family values.

What my parents would talk about is not what a kid wants to discuss. They'd ask, "What were you thinking? What results were you expecting from that action?" These conversations made me feel guilty, but what they were trying to do was to teach me to be more thoughtful about my actions. Their ideas and words had a lot of power on me as a young kid. The final blow was that my parents would ask, "What are you aiming for in life?"

I knew that if I didn't come up with a good answer, I wasn't getting up from the table. So I'd say, "I want to go to Cornell University," where they went. I'd add, "I want to be successful, have a family, and take time in the summer like you."

I knew that I had to answer their questions. After I did, my dad would say, "I'm glad you know where you're going. But if that's where you're going, look at your actions today. They are going in an entirely different direction. How are these choices going to get you where you want?"

That's the same question I ask leaders of companies today. If you're clear about your vision but your actions are taking you in a different direction, how are these actions taking you where you want to go? I ask my kids the same question. They are avid about their dreams, but as a father, I want to help them align their actions with where they want to go. There's value in thinking big and setting goals, but there's even more value in helping people take steps in those directions.

Developing Problem Solving Skills

We teach LeadYoung Trainers and Koaches the importance of developing a decision making approach to coaching. Everyone needs problem solving skills in life, but a leader's ability to discover viable answers is crucial. Therefore, we want them to learn how to do this as effectively as possible while they're moldable. Unfortunately, in our attempt to be responsible adults, we accidently retard this development in young leaders. When faced with a challenge, problem, or difficult situation, there are four common responses. Only the fourth is apt to develop problem solving skills.

Power: Adults who feel out of control often resort to yelling, verbal put-downs, physical punishment, or asking rhetorical questions, such as, "When are you going to grow up?" and "Do you want a spanking?" When this happens frequently, a child typically becomes either aggressive or withdrawn. Eventually, s/he becomes immune to the responses so that the adult's power must increase to be noticed.

Suggesting: A second option adults choose, especially when a child mentions a concern, is trying to provide solutions for the child. Your daughter says, "My friends won't play with me." You respond, "Why don't you go swimming with Brooke, or why don't you invite Angie over to watch a movie?" While your intentions are good, the result is a child who remains passive, dependent on other's ideas, and who lacks creative problem solving skills.

Explaining: A third option adults take in helping a child resolve a problem is reasoning. "You won't have any friends if you do that." "Your teacher won't take that sassy mouth." The child eventually views this response as simply another mini-lecture and tunes it out. S/he doesn't change and feels detached from consequences.

Problem Solving: A fourth and effective approach is to engage a child in the problem solving process herself. This includes recognizing cognitive and emotional elements. The goal is to connect consequences with decisions. There are three aspects of a typical decision making situation worth exploring: feelings, solutions, and consequences.

- Explore Feelings

Begin by raising the level of awareness of those involved. Suppose your daughter hits her brother. You confront her by sitting down with her and asking, "How does hitting Benji make you feel?" "How do you think it makes your brother feel?" The goal is to consider consequences.

- Explore Solutions

After you unpack some of the emotions, you'll want to brainstorm alternatives. You might ask, "What do you think you could do next time your brother bugs you?" "Okay, what else?" The goal is to come up with a few possible responses, not just "the right one."

- Explore Consequences

Now you want to evaluate potential consequences of these options. "What do you think will happen if you hit your brother?" "What might help you remember not to hit your brother next time?" Like Dr. Phil asks, "How is it working for you?"

Josh Nelson, our middle son, tells a story of proactive problem solving as a young leader:" We belonged to an athletic club that had a tennis program. I felt frustrated that they were charging us junior players so much to play each other on Sunday afternoons. Therefore, I formed a group that I named FoCo (Fort

Collins, Colorado) Tennis and called about a dozen people I knew. We played at the high school courts. There was no charge, but everyone was required to bring a can of tennis balls to play. The club ended up shutting down their program because people pulled out when they realized they didn't have to pay to have an organized hit-around time."

We'll wrap up this chapter with some of the bullet points we provide in our LeadYoung certification and coach training. They represent some best practices and common errors we've noticed over the years.

Dr. John Maxwell, bestselling author (and past mentor of Dr. Nelson), talks about a leadership training idea he's used.

You can never start too young in teaching a child to lead. My dad was profoundly influential in the leadership development of my brother and myself. He not only modeled exceptional leadership, but he knew how to invest in us individually to bring out what we needed.

One thing Dad did was something that I have done with our two children: paying us to read good books on leaders. The key is rewarding desired behavior. Paying your children to take out the trash is great if you want them to become a garbage collector. Paying them to make their bed or keep their rooms straight is okay if you want to raise a maid. But pay them to read a good book, perhaps a biography on a famous leader, and then have them tell you about it or write a report on it. That way, they learn about these people and what made them great leaders.

Two Key Percents

Keep these dual amounts in mind as you coach:

• 75% of teaching is Socratic. Avoid telling. Your goal is to engage young leaders in discovery.

• 25% talking time is your maximum "air time" allowance. If you hear your own voice more than one fourth of the time, you're talking too much. Learn to give up control.

Socratic Teaching (Asking Strategic Questions):

Think of yourself as a tour guide more than a teacher. Learn to ask strategic questions:

1. *Focus on the topic; avoid rabbit trail questions.*

Ask: What is one thing you learned about leading from that activity?

Not: How did you enjoy that activity?

2. *Consider options; don't just settle for one good answer.*

Say: That's good. Let's think of four more ways we could have accomplished this.

Not: Wow, great answer. Okay, the next question is...

3. *Look for teachable moments; great finds are found in failures.*

Say: We lost the competition. What can we learn from that?

Not: Oh bummer, you didn't do well. We'll do better next time.

4. *Avoid "yes/no" and rhetorical questions.*

Ask: What are some ways we can do better next round?

Not: Do you think we can do better next time?

5.   *Focus on the activity more than the person.*

Ask: If you were the leader, what might you have done differently?

Not: What could Josh do better next time?

6.   *Keep the feedback of people positive.*

Ask: What's one thing Karli did well as the leader?

Not: What should Karli have done as the leader?

7.   *Convey value for leaders' opinions.*

Ask: What do you think about how our team did in this activity?

Not: I think we did well, but we could have done better.

General Principles to Coach by:

•   There are no wrong answers, but there may be more effective ones.

•   Everyone deserves an opportunity to share; protect against time hogging.

•   Help develop good listening skills, not just good answering skills.

•   Reward desired behavior.

•   Remember the mirror effect; kids reflect what they see in us.

Mistakes of Ineffective Coaching:

- Telling/providing solutions/taking over.

- Failing to focus on the leader during activities.

- Talking too much.

- Allowing poor group dynamics.

- Lacking engagement; coach passivity.

- Lack of involvement among team members.

- Getting caught up in the competition yourself.

Positive, proactive coaching requires significant emotional intelligence from the adult. The benefit of consistently implementing this approach over time is a young leader who is thoughtful about problem solving, considers consequences, and is more effective in getting good results.

Hopefully you found these coaching ideas practical and reasonable. Many of them overlap techniques found in executive training tactics and "Love and Logic" parenting skills. Although the context focused on parents, they are suitable for others who find themselves interacting with O Factors.

In the next chapter, we'll be specifically looking at developing O Factor potential at home. Although sometimes dominant parents and siblings can stifle the potential in young organizational leaders, we want to offer an array of ideas of how to turn everyday family into opportunities to turn organizational leadership gifting into talent.

Chapter 10

What can parents do to unleash their O Factors?

As the twig is bent, so grows the tree.
–Greek proverb

We teach that LeadYoung training systems curricula are not substitutes for parents and guardians being involved with leadership development in a O Factor's everyday life. The goal of our training is to "set the sail," but it's the parent's job to fill the sails. The benefit you have is creating and taking advantage of teachable moments on a regular and individualized basis. These become fertile soil to instill both values and skills that will become a part of the young leader's life for good. The difference between a parent growing a great grown-up and being a leader developer is that the latter establishes leadership situations.

Although genetics and a variety of environmental influences shape the development of all children, including O

Factors, it's difficult to know how much parenting impacts any given child. In fact, research suggests that the same parenting style affects individual children within a family differently. Children with different genetic predispositions don't react the same to similar parental input.[1] Some studies propose that parenting variables account for 20% to 50% of the outcomes in children. [2,3] So while we all recognize the impact those who raise children can make, we don't yet understand how to measure this influence. Common sense tells us it is significant, so parents of O Factors should be very intentional in how they nurture their budding organizational Olympians.

Three Basic Ingredients Needed to Constitute an "Organizational Leadership" Situation:

1. There needs to be at least two other people involved on the "team."

Great life skills are numerous, but leading is about helping others achieve together. Being in charge of one person is okay, but there are far more dynamics for learning leadership when you have a minimum of three. If you're a single parent at home with an only child, you'll need to include cousins, friends, or others to expand the team.

2. There needs to be a measurable goal.

What is expected? Measuring outcomes is important, but be sure that the objective involves setting direction, organizing and/or accomplishing it in a new way. Even if it's a task as routine as team cleaning the house, you may suggest coming up with a new and more effective way of doing it.

3. There needs to be legitimate authority.

Although you're ultimately responsible as the parent, your O Factor needs to know that s/he has a certain amount of authority to determine how to accomplish the task. This is room to spread his or her wings. Try to be clear what it is you'd like your young leader to do, not necessarily describing how to accomplish the task. While this increases the risk of failure, it enhances the child's sense of accomplishment and empowerment. Being in charge creates confidence. It's not just a play on words that "managing is different from leading." Merely having your child follow the directions that you provide is not authentic leading. Give your young leader sufficient room to do something new; don't just perpetuate what already exists. Responsibility without authority results in frustration. As a child progresses, you'll want to increase his or her authority as s/he demonstrates responsibility.

Leader Cues

O Factors in LeadYoung training systems curricula receive the following ideas to use when it's their turn to be in charge of an activity. This is especially good for younger and less experienced leaders who may lack confidence or an awareness of keeping the leadership process moving. The main point is to spell the word: L.E.A.D.

Listen to your team's ideas

"Our goal is to… So what are your ideas?" "All right, what other ideas are there?" "Thanks for sharing. Now let's get a plan."

Establish the plan

Select the ideas that seem the best.

"Here's the direction I think we should take…" "This is how we'll get this done…"

Assign tasks

"Who wants to do what?" "Ashley, we need you to…" "Jesse, could you…?"

Determine the progress.

If things are going well: "Hey, nice job, team!" "Great work, (name a team member)."

If things could go better: "Let's work faster. Time is running out." "Wait a second. Let's rethink our plan."

Feedfront and Feedback

If your O Factor is young or lacks leading experience, you'll want to brainstorm ideas for accomplishing a task. This is what we call *feedfront*. One thing we've learned in training kids who are on the bubble or who may lack confidence in a leader role is to provide a few ideas from which s/he can choose. If possible, check in during the task to see how things are going, and troubleshoot.

"Mom, Sara's not setting the table like I asked."

"Okay, Jessica, why isn't she doing this? What would be some ways to motivate her to do this, instead of screaming at her?"

Most importantly, debrief after the project. Feedback questions are very important to the learning process, but they often get overlooked because we don't make time for them and they can feel anticlimactic to the activity. "What went well? What didn't go well?

What could you do next time to be more effective?" Avoid scolding or punishing. Keep the questions neutral and matter-of-fact, and be very affirming. Treat your young leader the way you'd like to be treated as an adult in the workplace.

Four "getting going," "feedfront" coaching questions to ask:

1. What is it that you want to accomplish?

2. What are you going to need, and what do you have?

3. Whom are you going to select, and what strengths do they bring?

4. What are some ideas of how you can lead your team?

Four mid-course coaching questions to ask:

1. How is your team doing in accomplishing its tasks?

2. What could you change to be more effective?

3. What can you do to help your team work together?

4. How are you staying focused on the team and not doing the task yourself?*

*This last question is important among young leaders, who often get sucked into doing the activity themselves and lose sight of how their team is functioning. Chances are you'll need to bring this up consistently so that leaders understand the difference between team leading and team participating. While leaders can perform a function, they must always keep an eye on the overall performance of the team.

Four key feedback questions to ask after a leadership activity:

1.   What did you do well as a leader, and what did your team do well?

2.   What problems emerged, and how did you respond to them?

3.   What is one thing you learned about leading from this project?

4.   What is one thing you could do next time that might make your team more effective?

Four key feedback questions to ask team members after an activity, while remaining sensitive to the self-esteem of the leader:

1.   How did the team do in working together?

2.   Did we have the right people doing the right things? If not, what could we have done differently?

3.   What did the leader do that was helpful?

4.   If you were leading next time, what is one thing you may have done differently?

Leadership Projects

Most of the time, a few good ideas are all parents need to get going. The following is a list of projects and task ideas that you can implement in and around the home to help you grow great leaders. A parent will have to use his or her best judgment in knowing how much assistance to provide in terms of coaching. You want to help young leaders get some early wins, but you also don't want to create a dependent relationship. Plus, we often learn more from our failures, so letting an O Factor experience a setback here and there can be a great learning opportunity if it is handled well.

Meal Supervision

Don't just say, "You're in charge of getting dinner ready." Give your young leader instructions for meal prep, including the following:

- You decide what we're going to eat.
- Do we have the right ingredients? If not, how will you go about making sure we do?
- When will we be eating? You'll need to check everyone's schedule.
- Where will we eat?
- Who's in charge of cooking?
- Who's setting the table?
- Who's in charge of cleanup?
- Determine who is going to be involved in the process: "the team"
- Who will do what, how, and by when?

Debrief.

* How did the team do in working together?

* Were the right people doing the right things?

* What did the leader do that was helpful?

* What could the leader do next time to be more effective?

Garage/Room Cleaning Supervision

Instead of saying, "Clean up the garage," give your O Factor instructions for cleaning or rearranging the garage in a way that includes the following:

- Who is going to be involved on the team?
- What needs to be accomplished?
- Do you have the needed resources to do this (e.g., garbage bags, paint, shelving, etc.)?
- When does this need to be accomplished?
- What is the plan for accomplishing this?
- Who's going to do what, when, how?
- Who is the best at doing what?
- How will you determine quality?

Debrief:

* How did the team do in working together?

* Were the right people doing the right things?

* What did the leader do that was helpful?

* What could the leader do next time to be more effective?

Landscape Supervision

Instead of saying, "Clean up the yard, pull the weeds, mow the lawn, or rake the leaves," give your O Factor instructions for landscaping by asking:

- What needs to be accomplished?
- Do you have the necessary tools and resources? If not, how will you obtain these?
- Who is going to be involved on the team?
- Who's good at what?
- When does this need to be accomplished?

Debrief:

* How did the team do in working together?

* Were the right people doing the right things?

* What did the leader do that was helpful?

* What could the leader do next time to be more effective?

Trip Planning

If you're planning a day off or weekend getaway, don't just tell the kids what you're going to do, put them in charge. Give your O Factor instructions by asking:

* What are we going to do on the trip?

* Who needs to give an opinion?

* How will you negotiate different opinions?

* What if someone can't go? How will you determine whether to go or not?

* How long will it take?

* How far away is it?

* Who's involved in the process, and what abilities do they have (e.g., driving)?

* What will this cost?

* Who'll pay for it?

* Is this in the budget?

* What do we need to take on this trip?

* Who will determine the map and/or get directions?

* How will we know if this was a good trip or not?

* Is there anything else we need to do (e.g., take care of a pet, pack bags, bring food or drink, buy tickets, arrange a babysitter, etc.)?

Debrief:

* How did the team do in working together?

* Were the right people doing the right things?

* What did the leader do that was helpful?

* What could the leader do next time to be more effective?

Adopt a Family

Whether it's the holidays or any time of year, why not let your O Factor organize the family and others to gather funds, supplies, presents, and goodies for a family struck with poverty, a struggling single parent, or an aging couple? Consider house cleaning, yard work, gifts, childcare, or any number of other ideas to provide support and care for a family in need.

Care Scheduling

When someone is having a health crisis or can use an extra hand during some other type of life trauma, offer extra help for childcare, meals, lawn care, or other support issues. Encourage your O Factor to find out what could help the person, develop a plan and a strategy, and recruit a team to accomplish the task. One of the biggest challenges is finding and scheduling others to help. This responsibility could teach your young leader the task of ask, a lifelong skill leaders must develop to be effective. Then helping volunteers follow through is a different challenge. Let's say the next-door neighbor just had hip surgery. An O Factor could contact the person to see what might be helpful. "Dinner would be great the next two weeks," the neighbor says. The child can then coordinate with family, friends, faith community members, and neighbors to schedule bringing daily meals to the recovering person.

Choir Leading

If your O Factor has musical ability, consider helping him or her arrange to become a children's choir leader. Consider a preschool group at a church or childcare facility. The organizational activities, such as getting music, scheduling rehearsal times, and working with adult assistants, help young influencers learn how to lead. Then, when it's time to perform, consider elements of marketing, event planning (i.e., refreshments, programs, greeters) and recruiting assistants. The young leader can grasp a big picture of the various elements that go into a single project. While leading a children's choir as an adult may be more of a teaching skill, as a preteen or teen, it takes on a greater dynamic of leading younger peers, working with adults, and building confidence with groups of people.

Coach Kids' Sports Team

If your O Factor has athletic ability and passion for a certain sport, consider how you might assist him or her to become a coach or assistant coach of an athletic team. Community athletic groups are often looking for coaches. For example, say your student is a little leaguer or avid baseball fan. What about allowing her to coach a T-ball team? Talk to the T-ball coordinator or a T-ball coach and discuss the idea. So long as there is appropriate adult supervision, leading younger kids is a great opportunity to exercise leadership. Most groups will have an age limit for coaches, but there's no reason why you or another adult can't be the official coach while allowing the O Factor ample opportunity to get experience coaching younger kids.

Family Budget Plans

Consider going over the family income, bills, and wish list for a month. Let the O Factor know what it will cost to "run" the family. Then let the child call a family meeting to discuss how everyone can best work within the budget, what needs or wants should take priority, and what should be postponed until the next pay period. In addition to learning lessons about income, expenses, and responsibility, your student will learn the process of negotiating priorities with limited resources.

Fundraising

Local charities are often in need of extra funds. Think of a potential community service topic that your young leader is passionate about, whether it's animals, the homeless, poor people, or those who are physically challenged. Find a local charity that aids this cause. Let your O Factor brainstorm ways of raising awareness and/or funds or needs for this agency. It may be something like organizing a car wash, going door-to-door for canned goods, or doing garage sales of gathered items from friends and neighbors. Consider letting the local media know, in hopes of bringing awareness of this agency as well as inspiring others to donate time and money. (Send news clips to info@KidLead.com.)

Game in a Bottle

The Game in a Bottle activity is similar to some of the accelerated learning activities we use in LeadYoung training modules, but it can be a fun thing to do at home. Most of us have a game in a box that we have outgrown or never use that takes up space in a closet. You can also pick up a one or two dollar game at a garage sale or thrift store. Get an empty 2-liter plastic soft drink bottle and put it next to the box game. Gather the family or your young leader's friends. Ask your student to be in charge of the team to accomplish this outlandish task: "Your challenge is to get the box game into the 2-liter bottle. Everything must be in it, but you can't tear or cut the bottle." Most normal-sized box games can fit. You can add some dynamics by giving them a time limit, such as thirty minutes.

Garden Planting

Let your O Factor supervise the family garden. This activity includes an array of tasks. These include obtaining resources and developing a budget for plants, tools, and supplies. Plus, there is research regarding soil types, moisture, growing periods, need for sunlight, fertilizing, and other horticultural details. Remember, for it to be truly leadership, there needs to be a team to coordinate for accomplishing these varied tasks. Don't worry about having a few plants that don't grow, because we learn more from our failures than our successes.

Gift Wrapping

Don't miss an opportunity to teach organizational leadership to a student and get some chores done at the same time. Naturally, you won't want family members wrapping their own gifts, but let your young leader work on a plan to lead the family in gift wrapping. Tasks can include gathering supplies, scheduling within busy holiday schedules, making a check- off list, and perhaps even doing some training and quality assurance.

Team Shop

Whether it's going back to school or grocery shopping, consider encouraging your O Factor to get some friends together who have a set budget, and then plan how to best use their money. This may involve some preliminary cost research, determining the best stores, and then shopping as a group while discussing opinions, making decisions, and accomplishing the task in a certain amount of time. Returns are a part of shopping, so teach responsibility by putting them in charge of taking items back in case a purchase isn't quite right.

Internet Biz

Your O Factor is probably familiar with the World Wide Web, sending e-mails, and other computer skills. Why not help your daughter develop a website that would involve others so that s/he can develop leadership skills of recruiting, motivating, and casting vision? For a nominal fee, sometimes included in your current Internet service, you can have a website that can be created with user-friendly software. Perhaps it's a weekly e-news service for students, letting them know what's going on in your community for families and kids. Maybe it's a "Dear Abby" advice column for selecting school attire, getting along with parents or siblings, or even a tutorial on some sort of skills. Perhaps it's covering news of a youth sports team or league. Your students can determine if they want to sell ads or get sponsors. Dream up ideas.

Leaf Raking Biz

Raking leaves is a great young leader business in parts of the country where leaves fall. Like all of these ideas, getting others to be a part of the team will turn it from an individual work opportunity to a leadership learning one. Who'll be on the team? Who'll do what? What will we charge? What tools will we need? Where will we get the tools? Where will we dispose of the leaves? How will we market the biz? What will the team members be paid? Who'll schedule the work?

Party Planning

Encourage your O Factor to plan a party that will be run by a small team of people. A variety of things will need to be considered, such as adult supervision, theme, food, timing, location, resources, preparation, cleanup, and communication. Take a backseat as you let the children run this event for their peers or other families.

Pet Care Biz

People are always looking for someone who can provide care for their pets, whether it's watering, feeding, and walking pets while the owners are away, or merely cleaning up poop in the yard. But doing this alone is not an organizational leadership situation, even though children can develop good qualities from this. But if your O Factor "hires" others to be a part of this team and recruits them to work, get new business, market, and be scheduled to cover the responsibilities of commitments made, then you have a leadership learning opportunity. Obviously, you'd want to check safety issues (toxic waste, local guard dogs, or unfriendly owners), but what a great opportunity to spruce up the community as your child learns philanthropy, team building, resource procurement (trash bags, gloves, refreshments, disposal), and responsibility.

Restroom Cleaning Biz

Who hasn't had a bad restroom experience in a local gas station or small business? What if your O Factor started a restroom cleaning service that provided daily care for local facilities needing refreshment? Recruiting staff members would make it a leadership opportunity, involving scheduling, managing materials purchases, negotiating pay, motivating, arranging transportation, handling conflict, and training. (Of course, getting your leader to start with his own bathroom would be good.)

Snow Removal Biz

If you live in cold country, chances are there will be opportunities for your O Factor to develop a team of people who'll remove snow, either for free for people in need, or for a fee for the rest of us. Recruiting team members, gathering resources (shovels, snow blowers, bags of salt, adequate clothing) advertising, setting fees, scheduling work, and handling all that goes into activating a team will help your student learn valuable skills and gain invaluable experience.

pre·co·cious: *adjective*
(of a child) having developed certain abilities or proclivities at an earlier age than usual

Hopefully these ideas are helpful to you as parents, especially if you're trying to raise a precocious organizational leader we affectionately refer to as an O Factor. The better you get at fanning the flames of your child's special ability, the more you'll enjoy the results as will your child. If you come up with your own project ideas and experiences, please share them with us via the KidLead website.

In the next two chapters, we'll change our gaze from developing O Factors in the home, to the most prolific single social structure in the world, the local school. While most schools could become O Factor-ies, very few are, because instead of raising organizational leadership giftedness in students, they tend to raze them. In the first of these two chapters, we'll focus on the reasons why schools should take this non-academic gift so seriously for the sake of academic achievement. In the second, we'll provide practical ideas for designing O Factor *friendly* classrooms.

Endnotes:

1. Maccoby, E. E. (200). Parenting and its effects on children: On reading and misreading behavior genetics. *Annual Review Psychology*, 51:1-27.

2. Conger, R. D. and Elder, G. H. (1994). Families in troubled times: Adapting to change in rural America. Hawthorne, NY: Aldine.

3. Reiss, D., Hetherington, E.M., Plomin, R., Howe G. W., Simmens, S. J., et al. (199)5. Genetic questions for environmental studies: Differential parenting and psychopathology in adolescence. *Arch General Psychiatry* 52:925-36.

Chapter 11

Why are O Factors key to school climate?

The Role of Thermostats

What are the top two things people complain about most at work? They think it's too hot or too cold. When you walk into a room that's too hot or too cold, what do you do? You check the thermostat, because that's how you control the temperature. Thermometers don't set the temperature, they just measure it.

My friend and former work colleague, Jeff White, is a brand expert and graphic designer. He developed the cover of this book to convey the title in the context of how O Factors set the temperature of their social environments. This metaphor is the primary theme of what we talk about when we interact with educators interested in our training curricula, because few are interested in serious leadership development and most GT programs focus solely on academics. Outside of athletics, schools find little time or resources to budget toward non-academic programs. Yet, in this case, they overlook a powerful potential for social engineering by identifying and developing the O Factors, who are the student Thermostats, setting the temperature reflected among the large majority that function as thermometers.

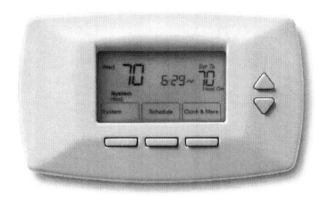

Anyone who has ever taught formally understands that the quality of the social atmosphere in a classroom, and the school as a whole, directly affects academic outcomes among the students. That's why organizations such as KIPP (Knowledge Is Power Program) schools can be so successful in very difficult communities. One of the first things they do is focus on the social infrastructure that enables good learning. Dr. Tom Torlakson, California Superintendent of Public Instruction, wrote, "Without a positive school climate, students will not benefit from improvements in curriculum and instruction, and reform efforts will fall short. 'All research… finds a positive correlation between better school climate and increased student learning and achievement' (Jones et al. 2008). School climate directly influences the cognitive as well as psychosocial development of students, promoting greater school connectedness, and engagement."[1] Torlakson states what all of us in classroom environs know intuitively: the seeds of learning grow best when watered and fertilized in positive psychosocial soil. Teaching and learning are highly relational.

Virtually all school climate researchers recognize 4 essential areas:

1. Safety (e.g., rules and norms, physical safety, social-emotional safety)
2. Relationships (e.g., respect for diversity, social support among adults, social support among students, school connectedness/engagement, leadership)
3. Teaching and Learning (e.g., social, emotional, ethical, and civic learning; support for learning; professional relationships)
4. Institutional Environment (e.g., physical surroundings) [2]

Because schools are social communities, bringing hundreds and thousands of children and youth together for extended periods of time, scores of supervised interactions occur. In the adult world, we readily recognize the importance of organizational leaders. We pay them more money than others, sometimes a lot more, to run our companies. We elect new ones when they fail us politically. We conduct sophisticated search processes to find the right ones who'll run our non-profit organizations. We also write books, offer executive training and advanced degrees, and pay consultants to coach them. Society understands and is invested in the importance of effective and ethical leading, but when it comes to pre-adult social groups, we all but ignore the role of these influencers. When we do acknowledge them, we don't know what to do with them or how to develop their organizational skills for good. Student Thermostats significantly affect the temperature in youth communities, not just adults in positions of authority.

Let me add a little disclaimer at this point. Some students can influence climate while possessing very few organizational skills. These kids may be socially popular, extroverted, physically attractive, talented, or even famous due to a parent or sibling. Occasionally, it's a lone bully causing peer fear. Their comments, presence, and behaviors affect others. Although O Factors can possess any of these qualities, what is unique about the people we're focusing on in this book is the ability to organize others, creating synergy. They possess a mission, a cause, a sense of direction, beyond what popularity, looks, charisma, or fear produce. So although we can't legitimately say that O Factors are the only ones who set temperature, they are the primary ones because their impact is more enduring.

Analyzing Social Influence

Example of an Influence Constellation for a Typical Classroom

(28 students: 2 main influencers, 2 medium influencers, 2-4 loners)

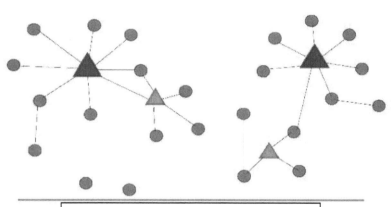

Graphic 5.0 Classroom Influence Schematic

Over the last several years, our pioneering work with 1000s of preteens and teens around the world, and those who work with them, has taught us a lot about how students socialize. In a typical classroom (Graphic 5.0), you're apt to see two primary influencers (larger triangles) and two secondary ones (smaller triangles). They provide a majority of the peer temperature control in a classroom. Depending on the adults' authority skills, students may dictate a large majority. Naturally, there are some who seem to be influenced little and who function as loners. The number of Thermostats vary year to year and are based to an extent on demographics.

Members of the Social Cognitive Networks Academic Research estimated that the social tipping point is when 10% of a group holds unswervingly to an idea.[3] Thus, if the student O Factors are identified and developed, the impact within any given school would be powerful. As adults, we all know that everyone in a group does not wield the same influence. The same is true with students. The challenge with preteens and teens is that they often lack training in how to use their influence well and/or constructively. To unleash their potential, you must provide concentrated skill training. Organizations such as schools that value conformity over non-conformity often reduce student leadership, confusing it with rebelliousness and thus punishing it, striving to extinguish these attitudes and behaviors instead of leveraging them for good.

Positive Behavior Strategies

Positive behavior intervention and support (PBIS) is a popular strategy to improve school climate. As an organizational behavior professor, I understand the importance of culture and how it impacts effectiveness. School climate is a big part of a school's culture, how people relate to each other, what gets valued, and how safe students and teachers feel. Although a lot of attention has been placed on safety and bullying the last several years, climate transcends these. A large amount of research has been done in this field, especially in the area of PBIS (www.pbis.org). So much evidence shows the connecting of classroom climate with academic achievement that the state of California now requires local schools to provide an annual climate improvement plan that's tied to funding. Over the past four decades, empirical research confirms that "positive and sustained school climate predicts and/or is associated with increased academic achievement, positive youth development, effective risk prevention, healthy promotion efforts, and teacher satisfaction and retention (for detailed summaries of this research, see Centers for Disease Control and Prevention, 2009; Cohen, McCabe, et al., 2009; Cohen & Geier, 2010; Freiberg, 1999)." [4]

The primary weakness in the positive behavior research is that it overlooks a key ingredient of student socialization. Researchers focused on the masses, but not the catalysts, the Thermostats. Dr. Jonathan Cohen and the National School Climate Center note this weakness as well. Their remedy is to include student leaders in the process of catalyzing climate improvement. "We can support students being our teachers; they clearly know something we don't. When students are integral members of the school climate assessment and improvement process, they can become 'change agents.'"[5] This missing link is critical, identifying the influencers and then releasing them into the student body as positive catalysts. This Trojan horse strategy is a subtle yet powerful way to leverage what is already available in schools, O Factors. By focusing on a few, we take care of the rest.

Typical positive behavior programs identify three tiers students. The 80% majority tend to be well behaved and receive generalized positive messages on constructive behavior and good citizenship. The 2nd tier includes 15% who are disruptive and need more individualized methods for positive behavior. The final 5% (tier 3) involve those who need more drastic intervention and who may suffer from emotional issues requiring counseling, therapy, and/or individualized disciplinary action. Although this is a very logical strategy, it is primarily reactive in nature.

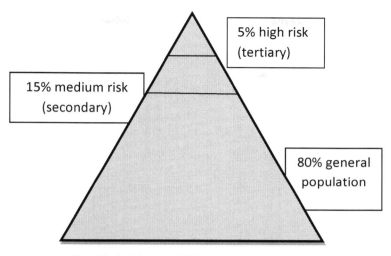

15% medium risk
(secondary)

5% high risk
(tertiary)

80% general
population

Graphic 6.0 Typical PBIS Improvement Strategy

A more proactive tactic would identify the 5% with the highest potential to catalyze positive peer influence. If resources prevented adding another developmental program, these could come from funding the 80% mass appeal. The result would be an overall impact on the 90% (95% tier 1 & tier 2 minus the 5% O Factors = 90% of the total study body). We question how much the O Factors could influence the 5% with acute behavioral issues, other than influencing the 90% on how to respond to the 5% requiring specific intervention.

Human nature responds more quickly to pain than pleasure. Therapists know that a client accepts therapy more deeply after a traumatic episode. Organizational change experts understand that people reject improvement plans that lack a sense of urgency and importance. Likewise, we offer Pablum to the student masses and attention to the trouble makers as opposed to identifying, developing, and unleashing the Thermostats. If we are to improve our schools as social communities, we must look beyond fire-fighting and focus on preventative measures.

An O Factor tier group, focuses on organizational leadership qualities, regardless of other behaviors, whether constructive or destructive. The goal is to invite them into training designed just for them, using project-based methods and Socratic feedback, modeled after high-end executive programs. We design such a curricula called LeadYoung Training Systems (LYTS). We'll discuss this in the final chapter of this book. While this type of training won't turn wallflowers into budding CEOs, it can raise the competency of your positive influencers and help negatives ones become constructive. In even passive, extracurricular use of the curriculum, teachers acknowledge decreased class disruptions and principals report fewer student office visits. An intentional, systemic application will result in much stronger benefits. Peer-to-peer leadership programs that teach prosocial behavior are recommended within most PBIS/climate suggestions, yet LYTS is the only curriculum that focuses specifically on the O Factors who function as social Thermostats in schools. It age-sizes organizational leadership skills development that until now has been reserved for high-end executive programs.

Mistakes Educators Make

Although we've noted basic ways that adults thwart O Factor development, school cultures commonly diminish students gifted in leadership ability. Here are four mistakes educators ten to make.

Mistake #1: Failing to recognize the Thermostats. Legitimately, most schools are busy, focusing on academic requirements. As a parent and a professor, I appreciate that. But most schools overlook a significant asset that's already in their community. Thermostats could extend their staff without burdening their budget. In an effort to treat everyone the same, they mistreat those with inordinate abilities. When teachers and administrators are unclear about who these key influencers are, O Factors go undeveloped and underutilized and can use their abilities negatively. Naturally, some are constructive, especially those raised in homes with strong ethics, but as most educators attest, this is decreasing. Even among school districts that test for gifted and talented students, nearly all overlook leadership ability. The US Department of Education notes that "most districts continue to restrict participation in programs for the gifted largely to those with exceptional intellectual ability. As a result they miss outstanding students with other talents."[6]

Mistake #2: Labeling Thermostats negatively. In our work, we've discovered that about 75% of teachers try to avoid certain Thermostats, because they deem them as troublemakers. Frequently, these students get sent to the principal's office for disrupting class concentration. While modern education of the masses requires a certain modicum of conformity, leaders by nature are non-conformists. Thus, we set them up to fail. Either we force them into their emotional caves with threats or we forever fight them, turning them against us, which is something you never want to do to a student with natural influence gifts. Playing tug of war with future CEOs is a lose-lose scenario for everyone, as learning takes a back burner to discipline. The world is populated with powerful leaders who tell childhood stories of demotion and intimidation in school. Many entrepreneurs testify they're successful in spite of their school experience, not because of it.

Mistake #3: Mistaking academics for leadership. Schools primarily focus on only two of the eight intelligences, identified by Harvard Professor Howard Gardner; namely, language and math-logic. While IQ tests reward those with elevated intelligence in these areas, many schools naively assume that these are equivalent to leadership. In our work with student leaders around the world, we've discovered that many (if not most) schools do not even allow students with sub-par GPA's to run for student government or serve in a leadership capacity. Administrators don't allow frequent flyers of detention hall into the extracurricular leadership class. Although some great leaders were stellar students, academic acumen is quite different from social intelligence. The "geek factor" is alive and well among many of your 4.0+ GPAs. Placing a model student, typically brainy and compliant, in charge of others is a sure way to damage the self-image of that student and frustrate the true leaders. One of the best places for your lesser academicians displaying social acumen is a leadership development program.

Mistake #4: Confusing student government & service activities with leadership development. I can't count the number of times I've had good-hearted, well-meaning educators tell me, "Oh yes, we have a really good student leadership program." After observing and doing content analyses on these, I've discovered that nearly all are little more than service-oriented social groups. Team-building exercises are different from building a team training. We estimate that half of student government members are merely popular, not organizational leaders. They get elected, but haven't clue when it comes to running something. The danger here is self-deception, convincing ourselves that we're producing leaders, when in reality we're turning out good citizens at best. Think of it as social math. Citizens add to society; leaders multiply it. But hardly any of the people working with student leadership programs have studied organizational leadership, led an organization, or experienced executive training. That's like an English-only speaking person teaching Spanish. It makes no sense. Another weakness is that we ask students to lead without training them how, thus producing mediocre events, clubs, and projects that could truly shine with effective organizational skills. This taxes students, staff, *and* community.

CCSS & 21st Century Skills

US Secretary of Education Richard Riley wrote, "Our neglect of 'gifted and talented' students makes it impossible for Americans to compete in a global economy demanding their skills."[6]

Schools, districts, states/provinces, and nations must analyze and improve the way they teach, if they are to keep up in the global village. This is very obvious in the US. Examples of these include Common Core State Standards (CCSS) and an emphasis on 21st century skills. Although these strategies are different from each other, they overlap. Teaching to the test and measuring memorization skills do not effectively equip students to thrive in organizations; certainly not contemporary ones. Higher thinking processes are needed so that students don't just follow directions, but can think for themselves. They must take risks and buck status quo. They need to matriculate critically, make decisions, and work well with others. This aspect of CCSS reflects 21st century skills, pedagogical strategies that equip students to thrive. [7] A benefit of organizational leadership skills training for Thermostats is that they are related to these strategic objectives, but now you're involving the social multipliers. Here are brief examples.

Critical Thinking: Organizational skills training using project-based activities focus on students striving to solve a problem with a stated goal. Brainstorming solutions, considering options, and making decisions with limited resources is the backbone of the training. Adults need to be trained not to provide solutions, but rather to coach Socratically, creating students who think like leaders.

Collaboration: Because leadership is a social art, activities should be accomplished in groups of 4-7 with designated leaders, replicating real-life team projects. Participants quickly learn the importance of gathering ideas, resolving conflict and seeing results in 15-30 minutes, allowing immediate feedback.

Creativity: "Thinking outside the box" is required when you lack resources (time, talent, tools, etc.). Creativity is rewarded, so long as it doesn't break stated guidelines, teaching the fine difference between coloring outside of the lines and behaving unethically. By emphasizing *what* vs. *how*, students learn to innovate. This is crucial, especially in cultures known better for their skills in copying others than for being innovative.

Communication: In addition to small group interactions during every activity, mini-projects result in one or all team members presenting their ideas to the entire group. Leaders thus learn how to convey ideas assertively to team members in an honoring manner. By adding final group presentations, students gain experience in public speaking, a shared skill among leaders deemed effective.

Leadership: This is included on most 21st century skills lists. By targeting those gifted in leadership ability, we significantly elevate peer leading among the very young, long before they'll be on the top of corporate flow charts.

Although all students need 21st century skills, effective organizational leadership training of Thermostats accomplishes both for your most influential students.

Paul Batalden of Dartmouth University said, "Every system is perfectly designed to achieve the results it gets." As a professor of organizational behavior, I agree. Schools are no different. Academic achievement along with teacher retention and satisfaction are directly related to the social climate of the school. Unleashing Thermostats, students possessing the O Factor, is a strategic approach to social engineering by tapping their influence. Even schools that do not prioritize leadership development should consider it as a means to accomplishing their academic goals by improving school climate.

In the next chapter, we'll offer practical ways to create leader-friendly schools that will help teachers reduce classroom disruptions and reduce the number of principal's office visits.

Endnotes:

1. "Safe and Supportive School Climate – School Environment" (CA Department of Education)
2. Cohen, J. (2012). School climate and culture improvement. In Brown, P. M., Corrigan, M. W., and Higgins-D'Alessandro, A. (Eds.), Handbook of prosocial education (chapter 9). Plymouth, UK: Rowman & Littlefield.
3. Social Cognitive Networks Academic Research, posted on July 25, 2011 (http://news.rpi.edu/luwakkey/2902)
4. Cohen, J. (2012)
5. Ibid.
6. Riley, R. W. (1993). National excellence: A case for developing America's talent. Washington DC: US Department of Education.
7. Trilling, B. and Fadel, C. (2009). 21st Century skills: Learning for life in our times. San Francisco: Jossey-Bass

Chapter 12

How do we create O Factor friendly classrooms?

Josh Nelson shares a classroom experience

I think that a lot of times, kids get in trouble for disrupting the peace and rebuked for sticking out. They get rewarded for blending in, but leaders often don't do that. I remember one time in second grade, I didn't agree that a girl in class was allowed to skip watching several Spanish instructional videos. Some of the other kids felt the same way. I got in trouble because I talked to the teacher in front of everyone, stating that we didn't think this was fair. You might say it was a small revolt. I represented a group of us that felt this was not right because she was getting preferential treatment by the teacher. The teacher asked me to stay after class. She told me that I showed leadership in the classroom, but I needed to "get along better with my classmates." (Josh earned an MBA and MRED from USC and is now an associate with a national real estate investment company in Las Vega, NV)

Leader-Averse Classroom Culture

Scenarios like Josh's (above) go on daily in classrooms

167

across America. I highly admire the heart and hard work of most school teachers and administrators I've met over the years. At the same time, the typical classroom culture is O Factor averse. The teacher's desire for compliance, given a class of twenty to thirty students, makes it difficult for the budding and often non-compliant organizational leader to constructively develop his or her gifts. Few teachers receive specific training on effectively handling students with leadership aptitude. Just as a nail sticking out of a floor is apt to get pounded down, young leaders experimenting with their influence abilities are more often reprimanded than rewarded by well-meaning educators seeking control of the classroom.

I realize that exceptions exists and applaud those professionals who recognize not only academic gifting, but also social aptitudes that deserve unique attention. While O Factors tend to be intelligent and good pupils, early bloomers are often not exceptional academically. Teachers commonly mistake academic success for leadership ability. As we mentioned before, academically gifted and talented students are often confused as leaders, but organizational leadership ability is distinct from traditional academic, athletic and arts domains. Sometimes those with high IQs lack social skills that gain the respect of peers. This awkwardness is often overlooked in arenas that reward good grades and academic smarts. A running joke in colleges reflects this principle: "Professors, be nice to your 'A' students because they'll come back as fellow professors. But be really nice to your 'C' students because they'll return to endow your program."

One of KidLead's goals is to elevate the education and training of those who work with O Factors, including teachers. With a little tweaking, most teachers can significantly improve the leadership development in their classes. The following are practical suggestions for creating a leader friendly classroom. As we mentioned in the previous chapter, this is also a self-serving strategy because when you begin harnessing the natural gifting of

O Factors, they will become allies and help you run the class. Miss these opportunities and you'll forever be battling troublemakers. From the classrooms I've observed as a trainer, consultant, parent and substitute teacher, I'm convinced that a significant number of disruptions could be reduced by creating a leader-friendly classroom and redirecting the influence of O Factors.

Ways to Create Leader-Friendly Classrooms

1. Identify the perceived O Factors of each classroom

The Pareto Principle, also known as the 80/20 rule, can be applied socially. Less than 20% of a student body will significantly influence the remaining 80%. As we mentioned, a typical class of 28 is apt to have 2-4 O Factors. The typical classroom will have 2 primary influencers (represented by the larger triangles in the graphic) and 2 secondary influencers (smaller triangles. Each class will also have 2-3 loners, students who seem impervious to social influence and who rarely engage socially. While specific classes vacillate from year to year, this is a typical average.

When we work with individual schools, we frequently do a brief training session with teachers, to education them on O Factors indicators and then brainstorm on a master list. We've found that with a modest orientation, teachers are about 80% in agreement on identifying these students. This activity provides a visual aid for everyone to be more aware of the O Factors in their school, along with being more conscientious about honoring and developing them. School staffs can use the SIS assessment to both educate teachers on what qualities to look for, along with creating an appropriate list of potential O Factors.

Tiffany Miller, a teacher who is also a certified LeadYoung trainer, says that she likes to start the school year with paradigm shifts. *This allows students to take organizational leadership roles and create a bond with others. This also allows me to see who steps up to the plate and who the leaders are in my room. I do a few activities that allow the kids to 'take over.' For example, I do a paradigm shift in science class to reveal you can think outside the box. The students are instructed to create a flying craft using only a piece of paper and paperclip. The goal is to hit a paper target. The inner ring is worth 5 points and the outer 1. If they miss the entire target, it's 0. Most kids assume that the craft is to be an airplane, similar to ones they have made in the past. I let them decide how groups should be formed. After each takes a turn to hit the target from about 5 feet away, they get another 10 minutes to discuss their new plan.*

This is when organizational leadership usually emerges. The O Factor usually selects the student whose craft hit the target, reconstructing that same one. Sometimes a kid will ask if it has to be an airplane. The leader is the facilitator. The only rule is to use the materials you have and be 5 feet away. Then a few create balls of paper and call them their 'aircraft.' This demonstrates teamwork and a paradigm shift. I use activities like these throughout the year so they learn to push the envelope and be creative in groups.

If you want more verification about a child's influence aptitude or if the student is new, interview parents about how their child acts in extracurricular activities, at home, and in the neighborhood. This will likely confirm your suspicions. Let them know you've identified their child as a leader so that you can team up to develop him or her. It's also a positive way to gain allegiance if and when you need to have a friendly chat regarding any class disruptions. Other potentially qualified observers might include religious teachers, coaches, or extracurricular program workers. The key is to find people who've observed students in social settings, especially where adult authority figures were not always in charge of student interactions.

2. Specifically invest in relationships with O Factors

While all students enjoy attention, taking the time to know the habits, hobbies, interests, and activities of your identified O Factors will go a long way in creating an ally relationship, especially when you need to ask a favor or confront an attitude. Although this may appear to be preferential treatment, everyone knows that in any given classroom, each student is not given equal time anyway. The key is how and when you do this. Figure out how you can establish rapport with O Factors. This improves your efficacy in confronting unacceptable behaviors if they occur. When teachers fail to gain the respect of them, critique and discipline are less likely to be responded to positively. Playing the authority card ("Because I say so.") is less effective with O Factors than others.

They're either going to work for you or against you. The better your relationship with them, the better your chances that they'll support you in your other efforts to shape the community of your class and school. Create excuses to have more frequent personal time with them, whether it's before or after regular class time. Even if you don't intentionally train them, invest the energy to get to know these students, their families, history, who their siblings are and their other interests. You can make eye contact with influencers and tap their shoulder as you walk past your desk. If you've created rapport with them, spread them around the room so that they serve as informal area influencers. Yet, if possible, seat them away from doors and windows. These are places of distraction. When a peer leader is distracted, others pull away as well.

3. Create roles of authority for O Factors.

Some teachers make the mistake of putting leaders in charge of watch-dogging their peers. Preteens we've talked to don't like this because it tends to place them in awkward positions of using their natural strengths in ways that alienate them from their peers, a.k.a. social suicide. Instead, make up activities or titles for kids with influence skills that seek to use their abilities more positively. Give O Factors special responsibilities, whether it's running errands, monitoring a class when you need to step out, or being team leaders for group activities. Not only are you helping them develop their gifts; you are also gaining allies.

This may give you more options if your in-class opportunities are limited and/or there is a class rotation, as in middle schools. Whether it's cleaning the room, removing bulletin board décor, or rearranging the desks and chairs, consider added responsibilities. When possible, don't just use the leader alone, but let him or her direct a group of peers to do projects. Adults may fear this sort of structure will create resentment among kids not selected. Yet most children will have little conscious awareness of this practice because they already recognize these kids as peer leaders. This assumes that the teacher has effectively selected those gifted in leading. Let these young leaders practice their skills. Be creative. Gather them to brainstorm possible projects in and around the classroom. If you see others expressing organizational leadership behaviors, feel free to provide opportunities for them as well to discover their talents.

This can be an opportunity for you to get to know them better, ask for suggestions, and brainstorm ways to make the class better. Leaders like to share their ideas and feel respected when given a chance to do so. You can make up a name for this group. The benefit is that leaders recognize each other. Even though these students may not be friends naturally, they will learn to respect each other. Since each influencer will have unique spheres of influence, this gives you greater coverage of the entire class. Relax and make it fun.

You may not have enough project ideas to develop the leaders you've identified in your classroom. Another idea is to talk to your colleagues about projects they might have. You could also talk to your principal, custodians, and lunchroom staff. Perhaps there's a neighboring vacant lot that needs cleaning. A school principal can do a lot to elevate the value of raising leaders throughout the school. Teachers who buy into the importance of leadership development can share ideas with each other. This is especially beneficial as students graduate from one grade to the next, when leadership-oriented teachers inherit young leaders who've been developed in the classroom of a colleague.

As a teacher, I see how few leadership skills many students demonstrate. Every day I try to find those kids whom I can help target their inner leadership ability. Not every child in my room can control a group or make the tough decisions, but I do have a few. These are the kids who draw the other students. When asked to move desks, these are the students who volunteer to create the seating chart. I asked the class to vote on two people to be the "leaders." These leaders would then guide the discussion and make sure the class was incorporated into the new desk arrangement. One boy led the discussion and made sure that not only the class agreed but that the seating arrangement worked for everyone. This entire idea was based upon one student's vision to create unity and leadership in the class. This by far is the best part of my job, developing their leadership potential. —Tiffany Miller

4. Revamp the way you do student government elections.

The typical way that schools conduct student government roles is well-intended, but naïve and misconstrued. Traditionally, announcements are made, inviting anyone who wants to run for student government, to apply and then conduct a campaign that mimics political elections, including posters, buttons/stickers, and perhaps a school assembly speeches. While appearing democratic, "of the people, by the people, for the people," (Lincoln), it's akin to a math teacher walking into a class and asking students what they want to study and letting them do as they wish. No accreditation or school board would affirm this approach to self-learning, yet that's pretty much the way we go about "leadership development" in our schools. The traditional student government consists of 50% popular students are non-leaders who get elected by lack of competition, and 50% who do possess aptitude.

Since I'd be delusional to think a simple mention in this book would be sufficient to revamp traditional student government elections, a savvy administrator could do the following:

* Create a list of O Factors, per advice mentioned in #1 in this list.

* Encourage members from this list to run for office, since many O Factors won't even think about student government

* Create an array of annual ad hoc roles that appoint O Factors to roles of authority. The reason for this is because if the goal is to develop a leader-friendly culture, not just fill a few positions, it's better to increase and decrease the number of roles, based on the number of O Factors identified. In a school with a student body of 500, you may have 10-20 positions in government. If half of these are occupied by popular students versus O Factors, you'll have approximately 35-45 O Factors who never get tapped. The goal is to fill students, not positions. Plus, you get around silly rules such as grade point and attendance minimums and good citizenship. These rules and regs keep many a budding O Factor off the grid and elevates a culture hostile to his/her development. If the number of qualified students ebbs as numbers fluctuate from class to class, then you cut back on the number of positions. The goal is to develop O Factors, not create a bureaucracy

* Recruit a savvy leader to head up this program, whether or not the individual is on school staff. Most educators are teachers, not organizational leaders. Find an organizational leader from the community, whether a parent or friend of the school, to team up with a staff representative and create a truly authentic student leadership program that includes ASB members, class reps, and the array of ad hoc students you recruit every year.

5. Connect O Factors with mentors and community leaders.

Invite adult leaders to interact with you and your identified leaders, whether it's at lunch or after school. This might involve a field trip with parents. Tap the potential of others who can speak into the lives of these future organizational leaders. By creating a simple mini-extracurricular program, you intensify your bonding with these young leaders. Plus, you position yourself as an educator who understands the importance of mentoring and organizational leadership development, raising your value among parents and administrators. Consider a leadership club for formalize these activities, but don't necessarily call it leadership, to avoid the baggage of who does and does not get invited to participate.

Do not underestimate a community leader's willingness to go out of her way to interact with your O Factors, so long as you convey the uniqueness of your group. You'll be surprised at the caliber of organizational leaders who'll say "yes" to your invitations, so long as they understand it's not just a generic class of middle or high schoolers. Corporate and community leaders tend to relate to and enjoy each other regardless of age.

6. Work hard at disciplining and not punishing O Factors

Although we've addressed this in a previous chapter, it's worth repeating again in the context of the classroom. While it's tempting to intimidate or embarrass young leaders who are resisting your authority, work hard not to dishonor them. They have a sense that their peers respect them, so when an authority figure tries to diminish them publicly, it will often backfire. Sending them to the principal's office, interrupting class to verbally flog them, or bringing significant attention to their failure will create an emotional barrier to you that you can't afford. While compliants will quickly respond to correction, non-compliants are apt to become passive-aggressive or aggressive. Either one is detrimental to classroom harmony and productivity.

We all have memories of teachers who made an impact in our lives. That's why many educators entered the field—to make a difference in lives. But when you change the life of a future leader, your influence has multiple effects. Since most leaders are not recognized as such or developed until adulthood, the chances significantly increase that you'll be long remembered when you see the potential in them as students. To make this difference when leaders are moldable is to leave your mark on all whom that leader will eventually influence as well.

NOTE: We have also created a free self-administered organizational diagnostic tool called the Student Leadership Development Assessment (SLDA). It is available on the KidLead website (www.kidlead.com). The SLDA looks at org cultural aspects related to developing student leaders. There are also numerous articles related to student development and research, at not cost.

In the next chapter, we'll look at the importance of identifying and developing female O Factors for the profound potential they possess for providing what organizations are needing today and moving into the future.

Chapter 13

Why are female O Factors so important?

All too often, on the long road up, young leaders become 'servants of what is' rather than 'shapers of what might be.' --John Gardner

Future Organizations Need Female Strengths

If someone asked you why women should be leaders, what would you say? If you responded "Because they're long overdue," that person might agree, but your argument would be unconvincing. If you answered, "Because women can lead as well as men," you'd also fail, because research shows that women must actually *outperform* men to be considered equal as leaders. If we're unable to effectively respond to this question, how do we hope to reduce the power gap between leaders who happen to be male and those who are female?

As of 2015, over 45% of S&P 500 companies' workforce are
women, but only 4% are CEO's, 19.2% board members, and
25.1% executive leaders.[1] Even though 50% of US citizens are
female, less than 20% make up Congress, and we've yet to see a
woman VP or President. The list goes on in terms of power and
pay differences, even though more women than men have
graduated from college over the last several years. Also, a recent
study evaluating over 7000 leaders on effectiveness showed that
women consistently outperformed men in 12 of the 15 roles
measured. Leadership consultant Jack Zenger concluded, "It is a
well-known fact that women are underrepresented at senior levels
of management. Yet the data suggests that by adding more
women, the overall effectiveness of the leadership team would go
up."[2]

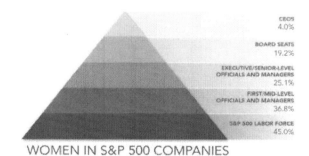

WOMEN IN S&P 500 COMPANIES

Sources
Catalyst, Women CEOs of the S&P 500 (2015).
Catalyst, 2014 Catalyst Census: Women Board Directors (2015).
U.S. Equal Employment Opportunity Commission (EEOC). "2013 EEO-1 Survey Data."

S&P 500 is owned by S&P Dow Jones Indices LLC.

catalyst.org

After 30 years of studying organizational leadership, I'm
convinced of one thing: the world desperately needs more women
leaders. I'm just as convinced that if we don't develop female O
Factors to occupy more leadership roles in the future, we're
doomed. I've learned a lot about leadership since finishing my

doctorate in the field in 1994. I've collected over 700 books on the topic, written 100 articles, a dozen books, and over 150 hours of training curricula. The last several years I've taught organizational behavior at the Naval Postgraduate School and Pepperdine University, and currently get to interact with many executives of large corporations in Southern California as the Los Angeles Chair of the Institute of Management Studies (www.ims-online.com). As I research where organizations and society are headed, my fear is that we won't see sufficient numbers of females leading us into the future. This is not a male-authored view toward feminism or equality, but rather a lifelong student of organizational leadership noting that the gender strengths of women are needed as organizations and society evolve.

Women Are Uniquely Gifted to Lead in the 21st Century

If we fail to understand and tap these unique gender strengths, organizations will grow increasingly sluggish and society as we know it will decay. Here are four primary reasons to identify and develop female O Factors, not only for their sake, but for the sake of organizations and society at large.

Social experts

Women, in general, possess stronger relational strengths than men. The number of social interactions and relational connections they develop are significantly higher. You can see this in everyday life by observing the way they converse with each other in cafes or waiting in line at the store, and measuring the length of their communications. Leaders are social architects. These "soft" skills, requiring social-emotional intelligence, are typically found in greater abundance among socially astute individuals. The task-driven orientation of factories and production organizations lend themselves to male strengths. But as organizations become more multi-layered and process-driven, other skill sets are needed. The

179

growing complexity of multi-national and cross-cultural communication means leaders must rely more on intuition, not just literal message content. High-contrast environs, where communication must be read nonverbally, lend themselves to the social strengths that women commonly possess. The authors of *The Athena Doctrine* noted in their research that if male leaders want to be effective in the future, they'll need to adopt many of these traits considered feminine.[3] Pew Research Center came out with similar results, surveying people about qualities they appreciate in leader, such as creative, caring, intelligent, ambitious, honest, hard-working, and decisive. This list was then used to ask people who they thought these qualities seem to be more true of, men or women? Once again, research points toward female strengths being in greater demand among leaders, now as well as in the future. [4]

Multi-dimensional

Women, in general, respond favorably to multi-tasking. We can see this in everyday life, in terms of how women commonly run the household, oversee child supervision, and work corporately. Some of this has to do with how the female brain develops in the womb. Hormonal chemistry increases the number of connections between the hemispheres of the brain, creating a somewhat different means of processing information responding to data. One of the results is an ability to respond to a variety of incoming stimuli, compared to men, who are often better at more focused, precise concentration.

An ability to respond to a variety of potentially conflicting needs reflects what is required as organizations grow in complexity. While current CEO/President roles in organizations obligate multi-tasking, these conditions will increase and trickle down, such that those better able to tap both sides of the brain and "spin plates" will offer superior leadership at all levels within an organization. This neurological disposition in women facilitates the busyness of business, without the overload that leads to poor decision making, frayed relations, and burnout.

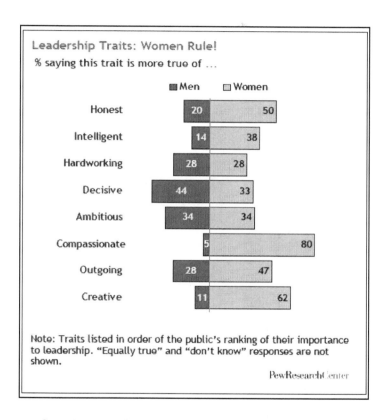

Graphic 5.0 Preferred Leader Qualities in Men vs. Women

Centric catalysts

Sally Helgesen noted in her book "The Female Advantage" that male-oriented organizations tend to be top-down, placing the leader in the highest box of the flow chart.[5] Women, on the other hand, tend to lead from the middle, much like the hub of a wheel with spokes emanating outward. This less hierarchical paradigm is more compatible with a world that functions increasingly democratically, with shared information and educated members. Centric-led versus top-down organizations catalyze idea sharing and communication, and tend to leave the leader less prone to the isolation that comes from the intimidation of position. This web-like leading style befits the flatter, more decentralized structure of organizations today that are likely to increase in the future.

Boundary spanners

Boundary spanning is an organizational behavior term referring to a team's willingness to go beyond its own borders. Because of the growing global village and sheer complexity of accomplishing goals, we must work with others outside of our team. The stereotypical scenario of the man never asking for directions represents the limitations of boundary spanning for males. Asking for help, reaching beyond our immediate turf, and integrating others is what is needed in the future. Women possess the strength of connecting with those outside of their immediate sphere of influence. Whether you're managing a Little League team in Scottsdale, Arizona or supervising an international project for a Fortune 500 company, the ability to connect with those outside of your immediate team is a strength that women bring to organizational culture. While this strength is relational in manner, it is unique in that it focuses on the ability to gain the expertise and leverage the network of those outside of one's own work group. Women are strategically poised to span boundaries as leaders, a skill that's required for both international as well as cross-team functions in today's and tomorrow's organizational complexities.

Carpe Diem

So how can we assist female O Factors to take advantage of the current and emerging environment where their strengths will be embraced?

Address female adolescent deferment. One thing we've noticed, both in our work with teens as well as talking to many who work in all-girls schools, is that young women with leadership ability often reduce their leadership behaviors in co-ed settings during adolescence. Perhaps it is a subliminal way to appear more helpless so as to attract the male's desire to defend, or just a way to avoid intimidating or competing with a young man she seeks attention from. Regardless of the motivations, this is something we typically do not see in girls-only settings. You don't need a PhD to recognize that regardless of age, both genders behave differently when they're with their own kind than in mixed-gender groups. This is a part of life, even when sexuality and romantic notions are not dominant. But unfortunately, this often comes at a time when young women leaders are also discovering who they are, how they're wired, and what their strengths are.

While we can't control our teens, because in their minds they're adults (and for all practical purposes throughout history have been considered adults), we do want to be aware when we see our teenage daughters pretending not to be the leaders they are. Helping them understand that healthy leadership is as much a part of who they are as being an attractive female will assist them in sorting through their emotions and behaviors during the courting rituals of adolescence. Naturally, we're saying this in the context that your daughter truly has high leadership aptitude. If she does not, that's fine. If you see her pretending not to possess the leader qualities you've seen prior to her teen years, offer encouraging talks and coaching sessions to help her understand that a young man who rejects her because she can lead probably isn't the type of man she'd want to have interested in her anyway. Sometimes, fostering her self-awareness in this area is sufficient to help her embrace her leadership during a time many are prone to hide it in order to gain the attention of males.

Seize opportunities. Research shows that women often receive fewer promotions because they do not go after new experiences to demonstrate their abilities. They seem less likely to embrace new opportunities than men because they feel the need to be confident that they'll be able to handle the new challenge (90-100% sure), whereas men take it on with a much lower threshold (50-60% sure). The result is that men accept the project and promotion, and for the most part benefit from seizing the moment. Since women are slightly more risk-averse than men, they pass up opportunities that can elevate them in the organization and demonstrate their strengths and abilities. If you see a project or promotion that interests you, but don't feel confident that you can succeed at it, take it anyway. Chances are the fact it interests you shows that you have much of what it takes to succeed, and the actual experience will afford the opportunity for you to learn what you lack and to make up the difference.

Create coalitions. There is strength in numbers. A team outperforms an individual in most situations. Therefore, women benefit from the power of a "tribe." Team builders are more in demand today than ever before, and will continue to be in the future. Whether it's a formal work team focusing on a project or an informal team you put together for breakfast, lunch, or happy hour socializing, gaining lateral allies gives you OPI (other people's influence). Lone Rangers get squashed, especially when you're a Lone Female Leader, so who can you reach out to (male and female) for the purpose of creating both social- and task-oriented teams? How can you help young female O Factors work together to create a club or sorority focusing on organizational leadership abilities? Even though it may appear more social and less formal, these informal networks empower those who are known and liked.

The irony is that while women possess a unique strength in socializing and relationship, the research shows that men are more strategic in how they ply their social wares. In other words, they go after friendships that can leverage their careers, either by opening doors of opportunities, riding coattails, or offering wisdom. Most jobs are obtained through who we know, not online job boards. You learn from what you do, but you get an opportunity to do those things based on who you know. Strategic networking is different from creating a coalition in that it focuses more on individuals and power and influence. My experience is that while women in leadership roles feel the burden of developing young O Factors, for the most part they're too busy to do this. I've been greatly disappointed in seeing how many are interested in talking about female leadership development, but how few are willing to do what it takes to identify and develop female O Factors. Until women leaders change their priorities and make room for the upcoming generation, we won't hit the critical mass to bring women into significant organizational leadership roles.

No one can mentor women leaders like other women leaders. To begin with, the romantic/sexual awkwardness of men serving as sponsors and mentors of dynamic female protégés lends itself to all sorts of challenges. But just as important is that women who are leaders understand what it is to be young, female, and influentially oriented. While leaders can develop other leaders to a point, men possess sufficient differences to limit effective mentoring of women. Just as speaking the same language is important to effective teaching, gender language differences make it difficult for opposite sexes to sufficiently mentor one another.

Hopefully we've expressed how important it is to identify and develop female O Factors. While we have significant culture issues to transcend, each generation will come closer and closer to empowering women organizational leaders to demonstrate their abilities and elevate the organizations where they lead. I hope that we can help fan those flames.

In the next chapter, we'll look at finding mentors for both male and female O Factors, an important strategy in developing the organizational leadership ability in students.

185

Endnotes:

1. "Women in S&P 500 companies," www.catalyst.org (Retrieved March 13, 2016)

2. "A Study in Leadership" by Zenger/Folkman, 2012

3. *The Athena Doctrine* by John Gerzema & Michael D'Antonio, San Francisco: Jossey-Bass, 2013

4. *Men or Women, Who's the Better Leader?* Pew Research Center (Aug. 25, 2008) *http://www.pewsocialtrends.org/2008/08/25/men-or-women-whos-the-better-leader/* (Retrieved March 13, 2016)

5. Helgesen, S. (1995). *The female advantage: Women's ways of leadership.* New York: Doubleday Currency

Chapter 14

Why do O Factors need to lead up & laterally?

The better the start, the stronger the finish.

Redefining "Politics"

You'll often hear adults refer to "office politics," the gamesmanship that happens when people leverage relationships to get their way. While students don't use the term, they are familiar with the schoolyard version. While the word "political" usually has a negative connotation—as in "He's very political," implying he's conniving, shallow, and manipulative— much of this process is related to leading in different directions, namely, up and laterally. Yet the root word of politics is *polis*, meaning people, community, city. The essence of politics is about relationships. As an organizational behavior professor, I teach my students that politics is purely a result of relationships; who knows who; who likes who. When you are on the inside of these and understand how they work, you're engaged and satisfied. When you're on the outside and/or don't know how they work, you tend to be critical and jaded.

Most leadership books are primarily about leading "down," influencing those who report to you or who are primarily in a following, team member role. I'd estimate that 98% of all the books deemed leadership fit that category. But there are far more opportunities to lead up and lead laterally for most people. This is especially true for O Factors because they have less power and status than older organizational leaders.

When you as an adult learn how to lead up and laterally and begin benefitting from these skills, you'll typically refer to such activities using positive terms such as networking, consensus-building, relationships, and shrewd bargaining. If you don't understand the process and/or have not developed these skills, you typically refer to them in negative terms such as selling out, brown-nosing, schmoozing, and being a teacher's pet. For the most part, politics is primarily relationships, taking the time and knowing how to establish connections with people possessing various types of power and influence. Understanding how to get along with others, trading wants, and accomplishing your goals through others' influence is all about leading—but not in the conventional sense.

When we fail to understand the dynamics of leading up and laterally, we feel victimized, blaming our situation on those in power or those better at something than us. By seeing a different perspective and training our O Factors how to lead this way, we'll provide a strategic set of tools that will benefit them throughout life.

Perhaps the biggest reason to teach O Factors about leading up and laterally is because that is what they'll be doing primarily until the ages of twenty-five to thirty-five, when most leaders begin leading down in our society. Quite often, those promoted to roles of leading down are astute at leading up and laterally. In other words, these skills will help rise faster on the organizational totem pole. Although lesser skilled peers may not like that and yell "foul," savvy organizational leaders realize it's a matter of knowing how to influence in different ways. The KidLead Inc. logo denotes this with four arrows pointing in different directions, reflecting that leadership is active and multi-directional.

If your student is not an O Factor, learning to lead up and laterally is even more important, since there's a good chance s/he will be doing more of this throughout her/his life than leading down. This is a strategic way of being significant in the leadership process without being the primary leader. Many people have made lucrative livings by learning how to connect those with power and influence. Even though I realize that this book is primarily for parents and adults who work with students with high leadership aptitude, understanding how leadership works is important for everyone. It lessens the chance that your student will feel like a victim as s/he gets older, wondering why certain people get to be in charge and get their way in social settings. This education is a type of power.

Backseat Leading

We also call leading up, "backseat leading." If you're like most parents, you know what it's like to have children in the back of the vehicle around mealtime. "Where do you want to eat?" you ask.

"McDonald's," comes the response.

"Oh no, we've been there too much lately. Pick someplace else." "No, we want McDonald's," echoes the reply. After a few more interactions, you find yourself in the drive-up window at the golden arches.

Were your children driving the van? No, you were. You

had the power to go where you wanted, but they influenced you from the backseat.

Backseat leading for students is about understanding who has the steering wheel at school, on the team, or in the family, and how to use that person's power to get things you want done. Sometimes it is as simple as asking. At other times it's being nice to that person and providing something they want, such as information, an offer to help, compliance, or even a compliment. There is nothing wrong with this. Knowing how to tap other people's power through relational skills is the key. Money investors refer to OPM, other people's money, a way to make a profit without risking their assets. Savvy leaders often get things done with OPI, other people's influence.

Sometimes you may not have direct access to the person with power. In that case, you need to know that person's "gatekeeper." Who keeps that person's appointment calendar? Who can forward a message to that person? Who is a friend, family member, or confidant who can put in a good word for you, make an introduction, or at least communicate an idea that you want the leader to have? Leading is about accomplishing things through other people. It is not wrong unless it's done with negative intentions. Since any of us can only know and meet so many people at a given time, we need to rely on the few who have access to people of influence.

The next time your O Factor comes home from school and begins complaining about the teacher's unfair treatment in class, talk to him about the idea of leading up.

"Honey, why do you think the teacher didn't let your team do its project in the workroom at school?"

"Because she doesn't like us," your student says. "Why did she let the other group do it?" you ask. "Because she likes them more," he responds.

"What if we brainstormed some things you might be able to do to let her know that your team would like to be good and use the workroom for your project next time?"

You begin a list of ideas that might look like this:

• Ask the teacher why she let the other team use the workroom.

• Ask her what it would take for our team to use the workroom to do our project.

• Say, "If our team works really hard today, would it be okay if we used the workroom tomorrow or with the next project?

• Offer to stay after school and help her clean the room to demonstrate support.

• See if she needs any errands run before, during, or after school, to communicate that I like her and want to help.

• Show that I am trustworthy by making sure our team's project is really good.

Sometimes, there's little difference between a person leading up and someone just schmoozing an individual with authority and power. The biggest difference tends to be in motive. If you're just interested in using another person for personal gain, then it is questionable, but if you're doing it to benefit others as a leader, then it's a matter of leading up.

Leading Laterally

The rook playing piece in chess can move up and down as well as sideways. The same is true with an effective organizational leader. Moving sideways has to do with negotiating power or rights from someone who is somewhat equal to you. This might be a sibling, classmates, or neighborhood friends. In the adult world, this translates into work colleagues, peers in a social club, and neighbors.

Lateral leading is relationally based and involves understanding the interests, needs, strengths, and resources of others. The commercial equivalent is bartering. Instead of one person buying another's service or products, two parties agree to swap different items having equivalent value. For example, let's say that you're an accountant whose car needs repair. You go to your friend the mechanic and say, "I'll do your tax returns for you if you fix my car."

"Hmm," your friend says, "your car needs some parts, so what if I barter the labor, but you pay for the parts at my cost?"

"Okay, that sounds good," you say.

The goal is to think of what the other person can do or provide for you in exchange for something you might provide for him or her. This type of skill becomes leading when it is not just for personal gain but is a part of a group goal.

How do you teach this to students? Your fourth grader comes home from school and starts whining about her and her friends not being able to play on the jungle gym because a group of fourth grade boys was using it during recess, and they always seem to get there first. You could tell her to figure out how to beat the boys there, or tattle to the teacher. But an organizational leadership skill would be to determine who the leader is among the fourth grade boys and then talk to him about either sharing the jungle gym, being included in their game, or negotiating a trade that makes sense for both. It could even be something as simple as being friendly to the boys' leader. While you may get a few "yucks" or "ooooo's" from your child, you'll be planting the seeds of how to negotiate as an organizational leader.

The same skills can be used at home between siblings and friends as a student learns to barter and negotiate with others in order to get what s/he wants. This skill is easily transferred into the leadership realm, where groups of people are striving to accomplish things and need to work among themselves and deal with other individuals and groups who possess power and resources that can help them accomplish their goal.

Social Banking

Organizational behaviorists talk about the concept of social banking. The idea is that all relationships have intangible accounts established that are similar to a tangible one in a real bank. When you and I come to know each other, I have an account with your name on it, and you have an account with my name. When I support you, prove trustworthy, affirm and help you, I am depositing credits into this account with my name on it. When I make requests of you, let you down, or offend you, I'm withdrawing credits from my account. I can make withdrawals until I am overdrawn. You may extend a line of credit and allow me to continue withdrawing based on my credit rating or your leniency in providing credit. The latter is often referred to as grace. But unless I begin making larger deposits than withdrawals, I'll eventually go bankrupt, and our relationship will end—account closed.

While social banking is commonly thought of in terms of leading down, it also has to do with leading up and laterally. An organizational leader creates enough trust and goodwill among others so that she can then ask them to do things (making a withdrawal). A young leader must first invest sufficient time, energy, and good actions in the mind of a person with power in order to make a withdrawal and ask for a favor. You can illustrate this concept to your child in a number of ways, from coins in a piggy bank, to milk in a glass, to air in a balloon. The principle is that you have to put some in before you get some out. The more you put in, the more you can get out, as a general rule.

Occasionally, you meet people who don't seem to ever let you withdraw. When you run across one of these folks, you usually need to move on because their deposit or withdrawal mechanism may be broken. By talking about this with young leaders when teachable moments arise, you'll help empower them to be more effective with those who have power and authority and decrease the chance that they will feel trapped or powerless.

The processes of leading up and laterally are significantly overlooked strategies in the field of organizational leadership. Yet, they are vital for O Factors to learn, since they'll be doing these the first 10-20 years of their lives and will help them climb the organizational ladder faster if they're competent it them. Yet, this needs to be intentional training because most books and resources focus on leading subordinates (down).

In the next and final chapter, we'll look at the importance of finding an organizational leadership mentor for O Factors, enabling them to speed up their development.

Chapter 15

How do we mentor O Factors?

Don't judge each day by the harvest you reap, but by the seeds you plant.

−Robert Louis Stevenson

The Power of Mentoring

In ancient times, as in many cultures today, the village setting allowed people to help raise each other's children. When tribal elders invested in young leaders, it created an organic strategy for perpetuating influencers. That's all but lost in America. According to Peter Drucker, known as the father of modern management, local communities of faith are the closest setting to this remaining in our culture. As a result of losing the village effect, we lack natural mentoring, where informal, non-parent contact is individualized. Mentoring is beneficial for all youth, but it is vital in growing organizational leaders.

Even though there is a touch of mentoring that we have designed into our KidLead training programs, where the trainer and Koaches provide individualized attention to young leaders, we highly encourage parents to seek additional mentoring opportunities. This allows children to interact with leaders in the community, who can leave a positive mark on a young leader's life. A mentor is different from a trainer, teacher, or coach. A mentor is a person who invests in a person individually, passing on life experience and wisdom.

Most of us feel a bit intimidated when we think of finding or being a mentor. Perhaps it's because we see influencing a young person other than our children as such an awesome responsibility. Maybe it's because we don't feel worthy or that we're just plain embarrassed to ask or be asked. More than likely, few of us have experienced a mentoring relationship, so replicating it doesn't come natural. Then there's the social awkwardness created by unfortunate cases of child abuse and molestation, causing responsible people to feel paranoid about a one-on-one connection with a minor.

But more than anything, the reason we don't mentor or pursue mentoring relationships for our children is that we're not sure what to do. We've made it out to be a big commitment spanning long periods of time, akin to a corporate internship or foster parenting. But this need not be. You can make a big impact in a short time with a little effort that young leaders will remember for years to come.

Short-term mentoring impacts a young life for two reasons. First, the one-on-one interest of another adult in the life of a young person makes a difference. Your presence communicates value, esteem, and belief in this future leader because it's not your job to do this. Secondly, adult experiences we take for granted, such as staff meetings, business calls, and any number of tasks related to our job as leaders, create a potent memory to a young leader whose life has pretty much been defined by entertaining media, family, school, sports, and peers. Don't underestimate the positive impact on a child sitting in your office, listening in as you call a client and watching your interactions with colleagues.

Our middle son, Josh, demonstrated a flair for business as a preteen. He'd ride his bicycle around our neighborhood, collecting "House for Sale" flyers, figuring out the cost per square footage and letting us know when there was a good deal or overpriced home. We're not business-oriented, so we asked a friend of ours who is an entrepreneur to let Josh hang out with him for a day or two, simply shadowing him and letting him ask questions. The man was checking out a rental property to invest in, so as they walked through the house, he asked Josh how much money he had. Josh told him, and the man asked, "How'd you like to go in 10 percent of a rental property?" "Sure," Josh said. So at the age of fourteen, Josh made his first real estate investment.

Awhile later, we arranged for Josh to talk to a friend who was a certified financial planner. The man ended up offering Josh a part- time job in his office, sending out checks and such. The man gave him a brief introduction to investing in stocks, and Josh ended up buying shares of a company as a fourteen-year-old. He's continued to monitor, buy, and sell stocks since. Josh, in turn, mentored Jesse (his younger brother), who became a stock owner at the age of twelve. While this type of mentoring is good for all kids, it illustrates opportunities around us to introduce our young leaders to people who lead in their work. They introduce expertise, experiences, styles, and insights beyond our own.

Mentoring is a powerful force in the life of a young leader. The following ideas show how to find a mentor for your young leader and how to serve as a mentor.

Finding a Mentor for Your O Factor

• Consider a friend or family member who has an expertise different from yours. Obviously, you'll need to use your head regarding logistics, timing, and trust, but don't let these details deter you from asking someone to do a mentor meeting with your child. Most people feel honored to be asked. You may even want to avoid the term "mentor," as it can be intimidating. Use phrases such as "shadowing you," "watching you work," or "spending time with you at your job."

• Ask the mentor to meet one to two times with your daughter for one to two hours each time. This need not be a long or protracted arrangement. It works best if this is done in the mentor's office or workspace, as opposed to a neutral meeting place where the leader is out of his or her leading environment.

• Provide interaction suggestions (such as those in the following section).This reduces the mentor's anxiety and provides some simple coaching ideas that will help the "yes" come easier when you ask. You may also train your child to be mentored by supplying him or her with some good questions as well. (We'll provide some later in this chapter.)

• Suggest a schedule where your child can actually observe some leadership behaviors. There are a lot of things leaders do that aren't leading. They eat, drink, read e-mails, and do any number of other things that everyone does. When a potential mentor asks what to do, suggest tasks s/he does pertaining to his or her role as a leader. This may involve interacting with other people, making decisions, checking on a big project, and working with staff. The best suggestion may be to simply allow the young leader to shadow the mentor through a typical half-day schedule. It may not seem exciting to the leader, but it will likely be pretty cool for the young leader. Provide room for talk time and unpacking a meeting or event.

- Thank the mentor, and then review the experience with your young leader. Talk about his or her experience and what the mentor said or did.

Eight Mentoring Ideas

Here are some ideas you can use if you are asked to serve as a mentor or, better yet, if you initiate a mentoring meeting with a young influencer.

1. Talk to the preteen/youth like an adult, a future leader.

Don't worry about "dumbing down" your conversation. Consider how you'd talk to a new friend or outsider who may not know about your industry or profession.

2. Tell the young leader what you do.

Provide a simple explanation of what your company does. Many of us do our work without thinking a lot about it, especially if we've been doing it for a while. Don't worry about trying to impress or entertain the young leader. Be yourself.

3. Describe how people function as teams.

How do you interact with them? What are the primary tasks of the teams and team members?

4.   Show her your work environment.

This may involve attending meetings, visiting a job site, or taking a look at your office. If needed, introduce the young leader to others. This esteems the young leader. It also models your belief in mentoring and investing in future leaders to your team members and colleagues as they see you interacting with a protege.

5.   Think of a problem you faced and how you attempted to solve it.

Don't worry about all the details, but simply explain a challenge to illustrate what you do. People looking from the outside rarely see the difficulties you face. Consider asking the protégé what s/he might have done in that situation.

6.   Ask the young leader about her goals/aspirations.

By showing interest and asking questions, you're esteeming the young leader. Plus, you're discovering potential areas where their interests and what you do overlap.

7.   Ask the young leader open-ended questions.

Instead of asking, "Did you think that was interesting?" ask, "What was something you thought was interesting during the meeting?"

8.   Briefly tell the parent what you did and discussed so s/he can review the experience with the child.

If you enjoyed the time, you may offer to do it again. If not, then don't worry about extending an invitation, and don't feel badly about it either. Some kids will naturally resonate with you based on their age, personality, and interests. Others will not, but that's okay. You've done a good job by simply being available.

Questions Young Leaders Can Ask Mentors

When a young leader has something prepared to talk about, it can help the child as well as the mentor. One idea is to write questions on a sheet of paper and place them in a notebook for your child to reference. S/he can also use the paper to take notes. This can reduce awkward moments of silence when either person is wondering what to say next. When you explain this to your child, you may want to encourage note taking. This improves attentiveness and provides you with information for a debrief or even a simple report. This can also serve as a neat memento for years to come if the person is famous or influential in his or her field. The following is a list of possible questions. We suggest selecting no more than ten, depending on the type of mentor and meeting and so as not to overwhelm either person with too many questions.

• What do you do in your work?

• How did you get into your career?

• When you were young, when did you realize what you wanted to do?

• What do you like about your job? What do you not like?

• Who was influential in your life when you were young and why?

• What are some goals you are trying to achieve?

- How do you help people work together to accomplish these goals?

- Can you explain a recent example of this?

- How do you try to solve problems?

- What have you learned about leadership over the years?

- How would you describe your leadership style?

- What are your strengths?

- What is one mistake you've made, and what did you learn from it?

- What advice would you give me as a young leader?

- As you look at the future, what opportunities do you see?

- As you look at the future, what problems do you see?

- What's one thing you'd still like to accomplish in life?

- If you could change one thing about your work, what would it be?

- What would you recommend I read?

- What would you recommend I do to improve my leadership?

Mentoring is a powerful tool that parents can use to develop their young leaders. Establishing a meaningful mentoring experience is not difficult. It's a high return on investment. Consider this LeadYoung book as a resource, especially for teens and young adults, to be read by both mentor and protégé.

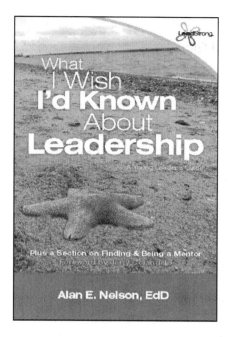

This book offers an engaging narrative, wherby a veteran leader mentors a young leader. There are also helps and practical advice on both finding a mentor and being one. For bulk discounts, contact the author through the KidLead website.

In the next and final chapter of this book, we'll look at what intentional organizational leadership skills training looks like and why project-based methods with Socractic coaching and debrief are key.

The O Factor

Chapter 16

What does effective O Factor training look like?

There are only two lasting things we give our kids. One is roots and the other is wings. This is especially true of O Factors.

Informed and Equipped

A few years ago I got a call from my sons, who were stranded on the road. It was a Saturday afternoon. They'd left home late in the morning to drive back to college in San Diego after Christmas break. Just past Pismo Beach, Jeff's 12-year-old car's transmission wouldn't shift. They called AAA and towed it back to Pismo, where they got a hotel room to wait for me to drive from Monterey were we lived at the time. I gave them our vehicle so they could get to school, leaving me with the lame car. The next morning, I was able to drive the 10 miles north to San Luis

Obispo, but then it quit again. I got a hotel that night until I could get it to a Pontiac service department first thing Monday morning. After a $100 diagnosis fee, the bad news was that the car was going to cost more than it was worth. It wouldn't shift into second and fourth gears. As I was on the phone arranging for a trailer to take the car home so we could sell it, the service manager walked by and said, "You know, you could drive the car home if you kept it in third gear." What? That's right. Third gear still worked, so sure enough, I drove it home. In fact, if we had that information before, Jeff could have driven the car to San Diego and avoided the towing, two hotel rooms, and a hundred-dollar diagnosis. But we lacked the information.

Information can change a lot of things. Most adults never seriously consider how they can develop the organizational leadership potential of their students. They do their best encouraging school work and extracurricular activities, hoping someday, somehow, someone somewhere will give them an opportunity to become an organizational leader and unleash their influence. But now you have that information. You know how to begin to develop the leadership potential of O Factors, students gifted in leadership ability.

I'm probably typical of many baby boomers who at midlife began searching for something more significant to do during the second half of their lives. I'm embarrassed to admit that my ego caused me to wait so long to launch KidLead because, well, I didn't think developing a leadership program for students was sophisticated enough. Although I value children and youth, I just didn't see myself working with them. But this really isn't about children or youth. It's about serious leadership, getting to leaders while they're still moldable. It's about impacting communities and governments and organizations for years to come by strategically growing great leaders. It's a matter of ROI (return on investment). Imagine what it would be like if we identified the high potential organizational leaders young and developed them early?

Analyzing "Leadership" Programs

As we mentioned at the beginning of this book, there are a lot of programs and organizations that use the term "leadership" to sell. With little official protocol in determining what is and is not legitimate leadership training, anyone can use the term as they wish. As a leadership specialist and organizational behavior professor, let me offer you a short list of things to consider when analyzing a program claiming to provide leadership training for students.

1. **Who designed the curriculum?**
   The first question to ask is, "Can I see the curriculum?" A lot of organizations just wing it when it comes to "leadership" training. That's like going to a school where the teachers just make up the lessons as they go. Is it written? If so, what are the qualifications of the designers? Most programs deemed as leadership are designed by people who are not organizational leadership specialists. Most have never been educated in the field, experienced executive-caliber training, or even led organizations themselves. These are basics when it comes to understanding and designing training programs that truly develop the potential in O Factors. Most programs are home-grown attempts to teach any number of things, most of which have little to do with what adult leaders who run organizations do. We talked about this in the assessment chapter. Well-meaning educators and youth workers offer their best efforts at leadership training, but very few reflect anything close to what executive programs offer.

2. **What does the methodology look like?**
   Many programs titled "leadership" use little to no research-based methods. Soft skills such as organizational leadership training can't really be learned in a classroom setting or by listening to a talking head. The best pedagogical method for developing organizational

leadership skills is actual leading, with individualized coaching. Project-based methods are vital to helping O Factors hone their skills. The goal is to not just turn them loose, but rather to offer a structured environment where individual coaching provides customized feedback to O Factors. Nearly all of the active-learning "leadership" training programs I've observed are about team building, not building a team. There's a big difference between bringing students together, helping them bond, and working as a team as opposed to training students on how to build their own teams. While the differences between the two sound subtle, they are in fact significantly different in methodology.

3. **How are the participants selected?**

A proverb says, "As iron sharpens iron, so does one person sharpen another." One of the things that makes talented athletes even greater is being on a team with other excellent athletes. If there are little to no qualifications or valid assessments used, then chances are you're going to have the "warm body" syndrome. Part of the efficacy of a program is that you've vetted the participants prior and made it an invitation-only event. As we mentioned, most student governments are at least 50% composed of popular students, not leaders, so even "leadership" groups consisting of popular election winners won't offer the quality of organizational leaders challenging their peers to get better. As in most gifted and talented programs, students go through a battery of assessments, including observations, recommendations, and survey instruments. The same is true for O Factor recruitment and training. A strong program is more like a competitive club soccer team, not a YMCA recreational league.

4. What are the qualifications of those doing the training?

Sometimes, people who design the curriculum are different from those who implement it. Therefore, it's worth looking at the qualifications of those who are actually working with the students. For the most part, people who implement student leadership programs are not trained in organizational leadership and have not led organizations themselves. Thus, they lack expertise in what it really means to lead and therefore, the training ends up being any number of things that don't really look like what adult leaders do. These training exercises may be service oriented, team focused, and character building, but do very little to reflect executive skills needed to lead others organizationally.

5. How are the results monitored?

How do we know if we're making progress? Very few leadership training programs for students involve benchmarking with pre- and post-tests. How do we know if we're improving unless we offer some sort of metrics designed to monitor growth? A quality leadership training program will include pre- and post-test instruments to measure results. "A good time was had by all" hardly suffices as a serious way to determine efficacy.

Vision

Imagine what it would be like if we could identify those with exceptional ability to lead, long before they became adults.

Oprah Winfrey as a child

Bill Gates @ 9

Ronald Reagan @ 12

George Bush @ 9

John F. Kennedy @ 10

Margaret Thatcher @ 9

Barack Obama @ 9

Hillary Clinton @ 11

Walt Disney as a child

If you're from another country, you could substitute your own national and cultural leaders in place of those shown here. These individuals represent a small number who climbed their organizational ladders. What might it be like if we found scores of people with similar abilities and developed them early, while they're moldable, not moldy? We now have the social technology to create programs to identify and develop future leaders for entire communities and countries. If we did this, I believe we'd witness the greatest leaders history has ever seen.

Our vision is to identify and train hundreds of thousands of aspiring organizational leaders around the world. To accomplish this vision, we'll need many people who desire to leave a legacy and invest in O Factors who'll be greater than they were. This includes trainers, coaches, organizational hosts, expert strategists, publicists, and public policy catalysts, as well as corporate and private scholarship providers.

In his book *Outliers*, Malcolm Gladwell reports the inordinate percentage of National Hockey League players born in January, February, and March. The reason is that in Canada, the eligibility cutoff for age-class hockey is January 1. That means that players turning 8 in January have more than 10 months of development on those born toward the end of the year. That's a significant difference at such a young age. Coaches begin recruiting the better players for the best teams, resulting in superior coaching, more practice, and 50 to 75 games a year. By 13 to 14 years of age, this advanced experience and resulting confidence are noticeable, and these top players are recruited for even more competitive teams and eventually the pros. Imagine what it would be like to give a 10- to 30-year head start to those with exceptional skills in organizational leadership!

I hope that you've been encouraged by the ideas in this book. I'm truly excited about the potential in a revolution that intentionally develops students gifted in leadership ability to be effective and ethical. We do have the power to significantly improve the future by influencing those who are and will be influential. I can think of no greater legacy than to leave the world in the hands of people such as this.

If you want to change the world, focus on leaders. If you want to change leaders, focus on them when they're young. – Alan E. Nelson

If not now, when? If not you, who?

-Hillel

Appendix

LeadYoung Training Systems

In the final chapter, we explained what a quality organizational leadership training program looked like for O Factors. The following few pages describe LeadYoung Training Systems, a robust, age-n-stage training curricula using principles explained in this book, spanning years 2-25, but emphasizing 10-18.

Stage 1: Formative (years 2-9)
Stage 2: Strategic (years 10-13)
Stage 3: Ready (years 14-18)
Stage 4: Ripe (years 19-25)

LeadYoung is the overarching name of the training resources. As we said, because organizational leadership skills are a soft art, they need to be cultivated with active-learning, project-based methods. These take place in concentrated short bursts, along with real-time coaching and post-debrief. Doing these over and over is akin to muscle-memory training for athletes, creating an eventual programmed, unconscious response in future settings.

Although the primary focus is teaching organizational skills through project-based methods and coaching, a secondary goal is to highlight 16 of the most sought-after leader qualities, based on a review of executive assessments and literature on leader efficacy (see Graphic 7.0).

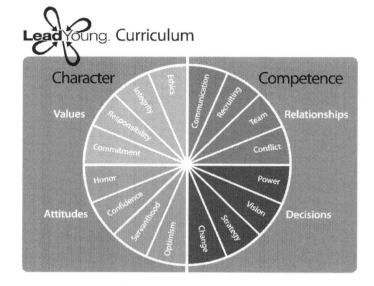

Graphic 7.0 LeadYoung Curriculum Wheel

The 16 leader qualities are divided into four training modules. Each module is color coded to avoid implying a sequence: Red/Ruby, Green/Emerald, Orange/Gold, Blue/Sapphire. O Factors can begin with any color of module. While all 4 combine to cover all 16 qualities, each can stand alone. A typical module can be run in sixteen 45-minute class times or as eight 90-minute after-school sessions. These can also be done in a 4-part, 3-hour weekend series or a weeklong, half-day camp format. After completing each series, we recommend practicing their skills leading projects or school and civic groups.

Participants take turns wearing a leader lanyard that designates them as the Team Leader of the activity so that everyone learns how to lead and participate. Each mini-project lasts 15-30 minutes, allowing a concentrated amount of time that includes problem solving, critical thinking, team member coordination, and real-time coaching. Then, each activity is debriefed as a team and the option of a one-minute coaching session provided private, personalized feedback for the Team Leader. There are various mini-lessons that last no more than five minutes. These are micro-lectures that explain a concept or provide an acrostic to give young leaders a more effective way of understanding the quality being taught. We also use kinesthetic learning through sign language (and a symbol for preteens) in order to strengthen retention. Plus, there is a concept card for each of the 16 qualities. LeadNow (ages 10-13) includes a Leadership Challenge to do at home, reinforcing the lesson and offering parents an opportunity to participate. LeadWell (ages 14-25) includes a book, since teens and older are conceptual thinkers. Half of this curriculum includes a strategic planning process whereby O Factors function as an executive team to plan and implement a large project, such as a school assembly, a charitable fundraiser, or something they develop on their own.

Teams typically consist of 4-6 students, keeping the adult to student ratio very small. The LeadYoung Certified Trainer typically functions as the emcee, introducing activities and overseeing the learning environment as well as overseeing the Koaches. A Koach is an adult who has been trained to facilitate team learning and is supervised by the Certified Trainer. A minimum size LeadNow or LeadWell club has 10 participants in order for there to be at least two teams, as most of the activities involve competing in order to simulate real-world pressure.

Stage 1: Preschool and Children's Programs

The first stage of O Factor development includes ages 2-9, divided into two sections: KiddieLead (ages 2-5) and Lead1st (ages 6-9).The emphases in this stage are conditioning and character. Through structured playtime activities, we'll help parents and educators identify young children with a natural aptitude for

215

leading and then provide program ideas for developing this latent potential. Although it sounds farfetched, those who work with these ages readily acknowledge how certain kids exhibit social influence behaviors. This stage offers an early orientation for leading peers in activities while taking advantage of character formation through role play, storytelling, and fun. This program will include a series of 16 storybooks shaped around the core qualities of our more formal training curriculum.

Stage 2: Preteen Program

The second stage of young leader development includes ages 10-14 (upper elementary and middle school). We've already described this in detail, but the leadership training curriculum is called LeadNow. The emphasis here is to target the 10/13 Window, when leaders are still moldable in their character but elevated in their cognitions. The name reflects the belief that preteens don't have to wait until they are adults to lead. They can learn to lead now. Another benefit of focusing on preteens is that they tend to be less distracted by hormones and activities than older youth. This is a robust program that requires trainer certification to use the curriculum, but can be done online and via video.

Stage 3: Teen Program

The third stage of O Factor development is ages 14-18 (high school). During this stage, the focus includes competence and confidence. Teens have become conceptual thinkers, so the type of leadership training they can experience is far more adult-like. LeadWell is the name of this curriculum. While it is similar to LeadNow, it realizes there are fewer chances to shape character based on the developmental stage—but can still significantly improve skills. Half of the curriculum involves developing and implementing a significant leadership project, since teens generally have greater opportunity to demonstrate what they've learned and grow experientially by leading projects in their communities and organizations in which they're involved. This program also requires approximately 30 hours of certification prep, plus running one module of the curriculum.

Another unique element of this program involves training teen leaders on how to give and receive feedback effectively. One of the things research notes about adult leaders is that they typically lack skills in seeking and accepting feedback on their leading. At the same time, they frequently offend and/or intimidate others because of ineffective feedback-giving skills. One of the goals of LeadWell is to train young leaders for a lifetime on giving and receiving feedback in an emotionally intelligent manner, in order to continuously improve their leadership and avoid getting stuck in bad habits.

The book "Lead Young" is for ages 14-25, focusing on the unique challenges and opportunities of young leaders. It is not "dumbed down," but rather reflects issues pertaining to their unique vantage point as young leaders, laying a foundation for early and later leadership success.

Organizations that work with students are encouraged to consider offering LeadNow and LeadWell as part of their development programs, if they are serious about young leader development. More info is available at the KidLead website (www.kidlead.com).

Stage 4: Young Adult Program

The fourth stage in O Factor development includes ages 19-22. LeadStrong is the program for this stage, emphasizing confidence and connections. Peek into nearly any executive training program and you'll see that 90% of the trainees are between the ages of 30 and 55. This is unfortunate, because so many O Factors have the potential for significant impact at an earlier age, so long as we intentionally develop them. The goal is to give leaders in this age a jumpstart in their organizational ladder climbing or entrepreneurial efforts.

LeadYoung Curricula Feedback

While scholarly, scientific processes are valuable, at the end of the day, it's often a matter of educators and parents seeing the results in their students' lives. Here's a sampling of some of the feedback typical of what we hear.

*We've watched Karli's poise and confidence grow. It's fun when she comes home from school and explains things she sees at school in the context of what she's learned at **LeadNow**. KidLead has come along and nurtured her in areas where we see her gifts. Now she has someone else to help us develop her and give us direction.* —Katie Klinger, Karli's mom

*My kids love **LeadNow**! They especially enjoyed the fun and relevant activities used to help them learn what qualities are needed to be a great leader; what a great investment in the future. The activities reinforced what they were learning and the Leadership Challenges were great.* —Margaret Morford, Jocelyn's mom

As a principal, I know how challenging it can be to run strong academic programs in addition to considering other enrichment programs. But I've discovered one that has produced amazing results: KidLead. —Diane Eussen, Principal of Benjamin-Eaton Elementary School, Eaton, CO

As a trainer, I am completely moved by this program. It has changed my life. I am a better parent, a better teacher, a better friend and a better community member because of my training and my working with the kids through this program. I truly believe in the curriculum and the success of it. —Nina Lewis, Trainer, CO

I thank you for sharing your program with us. With the help of KidLead, I hope to foster strong, ethical leaders today that will shape the future for all of us. —Maggie Schwartz, Principal Stratford Middle School

I have seen preteens and teens alike grab ahold of the leadership training at LeadYoung with great enthusiasm and put it to work in their sphere of influence! The next generation will benefit greatly when young people can lead with skill and competence! LeadYoung gives them these tools. -Nicki Straza, Trainer, Ontario, Canada

Leadership isn't a 9-5 skill set. Being a leader is a lifestyle. The sooner you can develop these skills, the better your life will be. KidLead and SheLead serve as tremendous resources for anyone looking to either ignite the leadership development process within themselves, or inspire the next generation of our nation's leaders. —Angie Morgan, author of "Leading from the Front" and co-founder of Lead Star (www.leadstar.us).

Leader Incubator

Leader Incubator is a licensing program whereby individuals and companies can run training programs using LeadYoung Training Systems curricula in their organization or community. If you'd like info on this or to become an independent Certified LeadYoung Trainer, feel free to contact Dr. Nelson through the KidLead website (www.kidlead.com).

About the Author

Alan E. Nelson is a social innovator. The first half of his life involved leading in the social sector, starting organizations, coaching executives, doing capital campaigns to build buildings, and writing books and articles. But after a decade of writing and teaching specifically on leadership, he came to the conclusion that organizational leadership training focuses on adults who are far less pliable. During his second half, he taught organizational behavior at the Naval Postgraduate School and Pepperdine University, while focusing his available time into research and design of O Factor assessments and training curricula. He is the founder of KidLead Inc., a non-profit org pioneering work with gifted young leaders.

Dr. Nelson has an MA in psychology communication (CSU) and EdD in leadership from the University of San Diego. He is the author of 20 books, over 200 articles and serves as the Los Angeles Chair for the Institute for Management Studies. He has been married to Nancy for more than 35 years. She is a leader in the senior assisted living sector. The Nelsons have 3 grown sons (Jeff, Josh, and Jesse), a daughter-in-law (Angela) and as of this book, one bubbly granddaughter (Juniper). Alan & Nancy live in the Los Angeles, California area.

For more info on Dr. Nelson's work or to contact him for training, teaching or consulting, go to the KidLead website (www.KidLead.com).

Other books and materials by Dr. Alan E. Nelson, Ed.D.

LeadYoung student training materials

LeadYoung Trainer certification materials

THE

O

FACTOR

IDENTIFYING AND DEVELOPING
5- TO 25-YEAR-OLDS WHO ARE GIFTED IN
ORGANIZATIONAL LEADERSHIP

ALAN E. NELSON, ED.D.

For bulk discounts on this book, please contact the author via the KidLead website (www.kidlead.com).

LeadYoung is for ages 14-25 and part of the LeadWell training curriculum. The last half of the book contains 16 short, readable chapters for discussion. Unique focus on issues that young leaders face, including leading up and laterally, how to tap power sources, and social banking. This book is also available in the SheLead series ("Leading As A Young Woman").

45 ready-to-use lessons on various topics, including a handout page with permission to copy and trainer page; plus 5 leader movies with discussion page; offers ideas for 5-30 minutes in staff meetings (8.5x11 inch format).

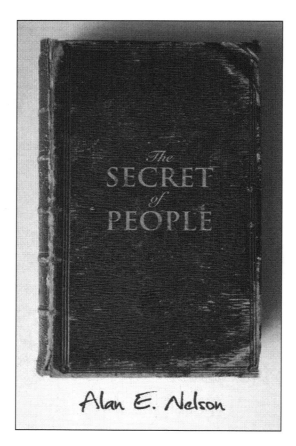

Although this book isn't specifically on leadership, all leaders
need to understand "The Secret of People" that is about
honoring others and understanding how to deal with them when
they're difficult. This narrative formatted story is easy to read
and engaging. Bulk discounts available, by contacting the
author.